New Directions for
Adult and Continuing
Education

Susan Imel
Jovita M. Ross-Gordon
COEDITORS-IN-CHIEF

Embracing and Enhancing the Margins of Adult Education

Meg Wise
ichelle Glowacki-Dudka

EDITORS

Number 104 • Winter 2004
Jossey-Bass
San Francisco

EMBRACING AND ENHANCING THE MARGINS OF ADULT EDUCATION
Meg Wise, Michelle Glowacki-Dudka (eds.)
New Directions for Adult and Continuing Education, no. 104
Susan Imel, Jovita M. Ross-Gordon, Coeditors-in-Chief

Microfilm copies of issues and articles are available in 16mm and 35mm, as well as microfiche in 105mm, through University Microfilms Inc., 300 North Zeeb Road, Ann Arbor, Michigan 48106-1346.

NEW DIRECTIONS FOR ADULT AND CONTINUING EDUCATION (ISSN 1052-2891, electronic ISSN 1536-0717) is part of The Jossey-Bass Higher and Adult Education Series and is published quarterly by Wiley Subscription Services, Inc., A Wiley company, at Jossey-Bass, 989 Market Street, San Francisco, California 94103-1741. Periodicals Postage Paid at San Francisco, California, and at additional mailing offices. POSTMASTER: Send address changes to New Directions for Adult and Continuing Education, Jossey-Bass, 989 Market Street, San Francisco, California 94103-1741.

SUBSCRIPTIONS cost $80.00 for individuals and $170.00 for institutions, agencies, and libraries.

EDITORIAL CORRESPONDENCE should be sent to the Coeditors-in-Chief, Susan Imel, ERIC/ACVE, 1900 Kenny Road, Columbus, Ohio 43210-1090. e-mail: imel.l@osu.edu, or Jovita M. Ross-Gordon, Southwest Texas State University, EAPS Dept., 601 University Drive, San Marcos, TX 78666.

Cover photograph by Jack Hollingsworth@Photodisc

www.josseybass.com

CONTENTS

EDITORS' NOTES

As adult educators, we increasingly risk and resist being placed at the margins of academic and other organizations. Margins, by most common definitions, are power- and resource-poor positions in which individuals are relegated to supporting rather than to setting organizational or societal missions. The power to marginalize often comes with a well-oiled set of connections to rich funding sources that reward the rigors of scientific method with its clean research designs and quantifiable outcomes. The power to marginalize adult education also comes with the power to minimize its relevance within the very social institutions that have wholeheartedly adopted concepts of lifelong and self-directed learning. According to this common definition, those with greater power place us at the margins against our wishes.

Certainly, no rational field of study or practice would choose to occupy organizational or social margins. Or would it? We argue that depending on how you define the margins, the answer rather lies somewhere between no and yes. Using the common narrow definition, adult educators resist trends to diminish the resources needed to accomplish their goals and influence their organization's mission. However, margins can also be a place of creativity and power from which to examine and challenge dominant ideology and practice. In this definition margins are in part volitional. This is evident by the people we choose to serve, the social issues we choose to address, as well as our preferred research and evaluation methods. Moreover, margins—volitional and otherwise—can be powerful observation posts from which to understand organizations from insider and outsider perspectives, span disciplinary or ideological boundaries that cloud creative problem solving, and influence change at the center. The cost of this hidden power, of course, is often marginal resources in the nonprofit, governmental, corporate, and academic sectors. But, we argue, it need not be so. Our tradition of (and passion for) facilitating critical thinking, dialogue, collaboration, and social change positions us to influence not only our organization's mission but the surrounding forces that set policy and funding.

This volume explores the margins of adult education from several perspectives; it then asks and addresses how to embrace, expand, and blend those margins by collaborating with others to influence the mainstream. Three concepts have guided our thinking as we first conceptualized and then worked with the authors to create this volume. First is a metaphor: adult education is a mighty river nourishing all facets of society. Second is Houle's enduring three-tiered pyramid (1956) with the creativity of the non-professionally trained adult educators grounding the field in social justice and civil society while the smaller tiers—the professionally trained adult educator in the middle tier and adult education professors at the top tier—

NEW DIRECTIONS FOR ADULT AND CONTINUING EDUCATION, no. 104, Winter 2004 © Wiley Periodicals, Inc.

support it. The third and final theme is collaboration, which weaves through this volume in several facets, and is by definition the nature of what one does at the margins.

Adult Education as a Mighty River

The river is a common metaphor for knowledge and wisdom. Whereas Hermann Hesse's novel *Siddhartha* ([1951] 2003) uses the river as a metaphor for the universal and unchangeable nature of knowledge as self-enlightenment, we visualize adult education as a mighty and ever changing river fed by tributaries and replenished by rain that carries the theoretical underpinnings and knowledge base of psychology, sociology, folk and cultural wisdom, K–12 education, philosophy, business, and so forth. The river of adult education shapes and is shaped by the natural geological contours, artificial dams, human and industrial pollution, recreational use, and the rural and urban communities through which it flows. Every drop of the river and its subsequent precipitation thus is a historical synthesis of all these influences with the potential to nourish all facets of the landscape—the riverbank, the watershed, and the recipients of its reconstituted rain and snow. As the river meanders though margins and centers, it gathers, transforms, and creates knowledge and influences all facets of learning in society.

Houle's Enduring Pyramid: Grounding the Metaphor

In 1956 Houle identified a three-tiered pyramid within the field of adult education. Adult education professors comprise the top tier. They train practitioners, in the middle tier, who combine adult education with other duties (for example, union organizers, workplace trainers, museum directors). Houle's bottom tier and largest segment of the field are lay leaders with little formal training, "who carry learning to their fellow citizens" (p. 59). The bottom and largest tier, sitting at many social and educational margins, often generates passionate grassroots creativity to build authentic civil society and democratic movements. Strength and creativity are fostered at these margins outside the constraints of, and often in opposition to, powerful economic and political structures. MoveOn.org (http://www.moveon. org) is a recent case in point. It uses the Internet to raise awareness of economic and political issues by providing nonmainstream news and analysis and to facilitate citizen action through political ad contests, bake sales, house parties, letter writing to opinion makers, and other pragmatic and creative organizing activities. It has become a huge grassroots movement for adult education and progressive political action.

Houle's model (1956) espoused a smooth and fluid dialogue between the three tiers. However, with increasing professionalization and the growing entrepreneurial paradigm within the academy in the intervening half century, the once central focus on education for social justice and civil society has moved to the periphery of the middle and top tiers' agenda. Moreover, to accommodate adult education's expanded scope and size, smooth and fluid dialogue has morphed into formal and self-studied collaborative arrangements. Through such growth and professionalization, the field has seen its status grow in competitive arenas, such as academia, continuing professional education, workplace training, and institutional support for adult literacy programs. However, such status must be protected from threats of retrenchment and has led to comparison with other professions or academic fields. Thus, the margins as a place of purpose and possibility are often equated with being marginalized—and thus a place of threat. This volume addresses both sides of this equation. As a mathematical concept, both sides of an equation are equal but configured differently. As a metaphorical concept, each side of an equation is often considered the other's opposite. The chapters in this volume express the margins equation as a mathematical rather than metaphorical concept. That is, creative adult educators can reconfigure margins (as power-poor positions) and make them equivalent to margins (as positions of power). We believe that there are many routes to balancing such an equation but that they share common ground through collaboration.

Collaboration: The Glue That Binds Us

The third theme that has guided our thinking is collaboration. Being on the margins sometimes implies being closer to the other than to one's own center; therefore, people at the margins are poised to collaborate. For instance, people living on the rural border between two states likely share more with each other than they do with people living in the large cities of their own states. Likewise, professionals at the margins of different fields who address the same adult-life issues may have more in common with each other than with their colleagues in the same field who address different issues. For instance, a health psychologist working with terminally ill patients likely has more in common with a hospice nurse than with an experimental psychologist working with animal models. Several chapters in this volume focus on collaboration across organizational, disciplinary, and religious boundaries.

Chapters in This Volume

In Chapter One Michelle Glowacki-Dudka and Lora B. Helvie-Mason review the literature that addresses the historical context and current thinking about adult education and margins. The rest of the chapters are organized along Houle's pyramid (1956). Three chapters address the bottom tier—social change and social justice projects enacted by citizen-level movements. They identify how our long familiarity with the margins positions us to project our mission and use our skills to facilitate collaboration that promotes transformative learning and social responsibility. One chapter addresses the margins encountered in the middle tier, using the example of a profession-ally trained human resource developer–adult educator in the corporate workplace. Three chapters address different facets of margins within the academy (the top tier of Houle's pyramid).

In Chapter Two Alan B. Knox sets a broad and far-reaching vision for future directions in adult education. Drawing on findings that about a quar-ter of the adult population in the United States identifies itself as cultural creatives who espouse lifelong learning, a better environment, and other progressive values of democratic civil society, Knox outlines a national col-laborative project across adult education professional organizations, uni-versity departments, and community organizations to advance democratic social change. He describes five projects that address specific concerns of civil society.

In Chapter Three Nadira K. Charaniya and Jane West Walsh, two reli-gious and adult educators, one a Muslim and one a Jew, describe their per-sonal experience with interreligious dialogue. They first situate their experience within the current discourse about religious identity in the United States. They then refer to the adult education research to explore the nature of learning that occurs when Christians, Muslims, and Jews learn across bor-ders of religious difference. Finally, they reflect on how this topic moved from the margins to the center of social discourse after September 11, 2001. In light of this, they challenge the field to expand the margins of research and prac-tice to include religion as a legitimate pathway to explore identity and culture.

Desi Larson in Chapter Four describes a parenting program in a rural community with high unemployment. This program used an emancipatory educational approach for people at the margins to develop their own learn-ing agenda, which Larson then contrasts with the mainstream skills-oriented education model used for people occupying marginal positions in society.

At Houle's middle tier (1956), Daniela Truty reflects in Chapter Five on her experience of living at the confluence of two marginalized fields. A human resource development (HRD) professional and an adult educator, she facilitated and then became a victim of a corporate downsizing action. She examines the paradoxes of perceived power from what she describes as a comfortably paid but relatively power-poor position of HRD, as well as issues of self-deception and the potential for creating change from the inside.

The next three chapters address margins within the academy. Sherwood Smith observes in Chapter Six the contradictions of having simultaneous insider and outsider status. He examines issues of tokenism, isolation, and the mainstream's assumptions of African American competence. He also provides a historical context for how, over the past decade, African Ameri-can adult education faculty created power at the margin of mainstream adult education institutions, which in turn began to shift the dialogue and agenda in research scholarship.

The next two chapters address issues for adult education within the academy as the paradigm has shifted from the liberal ivory tower (learning for its own sake) to the entrepreneurial research enterprise (attracting extramural research and other funding). These chapters address experiences from the traditional academic department and newer roles as collaborators work across departments and interdisciplinary research institutes.

In Chapter Seven Paul J. Ilsley acknowledges that no program is safe from threat in today's university. He then goes on to consider how the various missions of adult education are good for the business of higher education and critical to the academy. He provides insight into the savvy and leadership within thriving adult education programs—with specific emphasis on leadership in faculty governance and on significant partnerships with government, business, and community institutions that can create innovative programs that advance the university's future.

Meg Wise and Betta Owens address in Chapter Nine the increasing pressure to garner extramural funding for cutting-edge, interdisciplinary research. They describe how other fields have collaborated to create a new research area on the ways in which adults learn in the face of life-threatening illness. They use a case example of a research center that develops and evaluates Web-based programs. They conclude with suggestions on how adult education can contribute and collaborate in facilitating adult learning for this universal and transformative adult-lifespan event.

In Chapter Nine we conclude by summarizing the key themes developed throughout this volume, proposing multiple pathways to embrace and expand beyond the margins of adult education, and posing questions for future consideration.

In sum, these essays examine how adult educators collaborate in many contexts—how they negotiate power and maintain their mission in the face of compromise and how they continuously redraw the map of shifting margins and mainstream assumptions. We hope you find them thought provoking and motivational.

Meg Wise
Michelle Glowacki-Dudka
Editors

References

Hesse, H. *Siddhartha.* New York: Penguin, 2003. (Originally published 1951.)
Houle, C. "The Development of Leadership." Chap. 4 in *Liberal Adult Education.* White Plains, N.Y.: Fund for Adult Education, 1956.

MEG WISE is an assistant scientist for the CHESS project at the Center for Health Systems Research and Analysis, University of Wisconsin–Madison.

MICHELLE GLOWACKI-DUDKA is an assistant professor of Adult, Higher, and Community Education at Ball State University.

1

This chapter reviews the literature related to the historical, philosophical, and contextual issues that frame why adult education sits at the margins of the academy and society.

Adult Education at the Margins: A Literature Review

Michelle Glowacki-Dudka, Lora B. Helvie-Mason

Adult education as a field has a complex history, with roots in social movements and concurrent pressures to formalize the process of vocational education. This chapter situates adult education at the margins within academic disciplines and as an educational vocation. We draw on literature from within adult education, as well as reflecting on the broader social context.

Historical Underpinnings

A recognized literary foundation for the field of adult education in the United States is Lindeman's work *The Meaning of Adult Education,* first published in 1926. Lindeman defines adult education as the place "where vocational education leaves off. Its purpose is to put meaning into the whole of life" (1926, p. 5). He explains that adult education "will be via the route of situations, not subjects," that the "resource of highest value in adult education is the learner's experience," and that "authoritative teaching, examinations which preclude original thinking, rigid pedagogical formulae–all have no place in adult education" (p. 6). Adult education is "friends educating each other." With these guiding assumptions, the field of adult education shook off traditional methods of teaching and learning and assumed a position at the margins from the beginning.

These ideas, emerging from pressures on teachers to support vocational education and to carry the work of the university into the workplace, took shape in formal courses of study beginning in 1918 with adult education methodologies taught at Columbia University. In 1930 Columbia established

NEW DIRECTIONS FOR ADULT AND CONTINUING EDUCATION, no. 104, Winter 2004 © Wiley Periodicals, Inc.

the first department of adult education, and since that time adult education has grown as a field of study (Milton, Watkins, Studdard, and Burch, 2003). In the year 2000, departments of adult, continuing, and community education existed in seventy-four institutions in the United States, with thirty-eight doctoral programs and seventy-two master's degrees offered (*Peterson's,* 2000). Yet with tightening budgets and shifting priorities, the number of institutions offering adult education degrees has decreased by 29 percent between 1992 and 2002 (Milton, Watkins, Studdard, and Burch, 2003).

The field of adult education consists of three tiers of leadership (Houle, 1956). At the top of the pyramid sit the adult education professionals who work in academia or other settings; they are primarily concerned with the field itself. The next tier includes professionals whose duties include adult education (for example, nurse educators, librarians, museum directors, and workplace coordinators). The largest group of adult educators is made up of the lay educators (practitioners) who serve adults directly and may not even recognize that a specific discipline of adult education exists (Imel, Brockett, and James, 2000). This group includes community workers, training staffs, union activists, and so on (Houle, 1956).

Recognizing the field's leadership dynamics, Houle (1956) suggested that academic programs should prepare the field professionals (those who will be professors) to work with the second and third levels of educators as a central responsibility. Thus, the debate around professionalization of the field began.

In 1962 Knowles noted that as adult education becomes increasingly recognized as a discrete activity, adult educators in each segment of the field look to other adult educators as allies in a national struggle for recognition, power, and financial support. He explained that "the marginality of the adult educational role in most institutional settings induces an era to seek mutual support, status, and problem-solving help across institutional lines" (p. 265). Yet as adult educators work across these institutional boundaries and welcome multiple disciplines, philosophies, and methods into the field, they can become confused about the balance between their roles as educators and as representatives of their disciplines. Because adult education casts a wide net, professionals and practitioners must balance philosophical agendas, social pressures, and competing educational goals.

Historically, adult education trends reflect changes in society, from the social action movements of the 1920s to federally sponsored programs in the 1930s, from the GI bill in the 1940s to the civil rights movement in the 1960s. The term *lifelong learning* emerged in the 1960s with intentions to integrate adult education into wider public policy (Stubblefield and Keane, 1989). Since then government and business have used the concept of lifelong learning to signify constant retraining for vocational changes, rather than the original intent to value voluntary learning across the lifespan (Collins, 1991).

Purposes of Adult Education

Adult education mirrors and at times facilitates change in society, as Beder (1989, p. 37) explained with the "basic purposes of Adult Education":

1. To facilitate change in a dynamic society
2. To support and maintain a good social order
3. To promote productivity
4. To enhance personal growth

Although these purposes are at times contradictory, they accurately reflect the roles that adult education takes on in the United States. The location and context of adult learning may assign each of these goals to mainstream or marginal positions. For example, adult education programs in the workplace will mainstream the goals of productivity and support of the social order but may marginalize goals for personal growth and social change. A political action committee may mainstream the social change agenda while setting the others at the margins. A religious institution or health club may make personal growth the focus and marginalize productivity.

Currently the adult education field within academia focuses on issues related to continuing education, community education, adult basic education (English as a second language and literacy), lifelong learning, human resource development and training, as well as critical education issues related to identity politics (race, class, gender, and so on). The field of adult education also includes methods of social research (qualitative and quantitative), educational leadership, and uses of educational technology to support teaching and learning, among others (Knox, 1993; Merriam and Cunningham, 1989; Hayes and Wilson, 2000).

Adult Education at the Margins

"One must recognize that adult education programs are often marginalized within the academic institutions and often within the very colleges and departments in which they exist" (Imel, Brockett, and James, 2000, p. 634). At recent meetings of their professional groups, the American Association for Adult and Continuing Education, the Commission of Professors of Adult Education, and the Adult Education Research Conference have considered as a leading topic the theme of how to integrate adult education within colleges of education and at the same time keep its own identity. Milton, Watkins, Studdard, and Burch (2003) suggest that program integration (which they define as "the integration of adult education into the main focus of education," p. 37), responsiveness to change, and internal leadership are key factors in the strength and wellness of adult education programs. Although "deans don't support what they don't understand," these scholars write (p. 38), it is up to the adult education faculty members to educate their colleagues and administration in higher education to demonstrate and articulate the value of adult education.

The perception of marginal status stems from the lack of specific credentials for entrance to the field and from the ambiguous definition of adult education. Although scholars often repeat the arguments for and against certification in adult education (James, 1992; White, 1992; Boshier, 1988; Galbraith and Gilley, 1985), Boshier (1988, p. 69) strongly suggests that although "profound dangers [are] associated with training people along 'specific and rigid' lines," adult educators need training in program planning and teaching adults. These two topics are often at the core of graduate studies in adult education along with historical, philosophical, and sociological foundations and an overview of educational research (Knowles, 1988; Commission of Professors, 1988). Other issues of race, gender, and class certainly fit into the adult education curriculum. Therefore, the question of what the credentials in adult education are can be partially answered by looking at the graduate degrees available.

Adult Education as a Profession

The debate over whether adult education should be professionalized continues today with leaders in the field still disagreeing. Some argue that professionalism contributes to improved practice; others see professionalism "narrowing the parameters as to who can practice and what defines 'good practice'" (Merriam and Brockett, 1997, p. 220). Collins (1992, pp. 41–42) invites us to "place emancipatory interests above the technical rationality" and "to counter this apolitical professionalizing tendency" by "incorporating a questioning of all authoritative, professional assumptions into our pedagogy."

Although adult education is an academic discipline and professional field, the adult education faculty follows certain standards and attempts to fit into the status quo in order to hold status within the university and with other professions. Now in 2004 adult education has become a legitimate field of study with many graduate programs, thousands of graduates, and hundreds of books and articles being published each year for both academicians and practitioners (Griffith, 1992). Although it remains a stepchild to more dominant, better-funded programs such as K-12 education, educational administration, and human resources, it is a recognized field (Sticht, 2001). In the 1980s the concept of lifelong learning helped to push adult education into the limelight, and other disciplines took it up to forward their own agendas (for example, workforce development, just-in-time education). The term was written into grants in order to sell adult education as a product; thus, "lifelong learning as a guiding principle became a debased currency" (Collins, 1991, p. 7). As other disciplines adopted this idea, adult education returned to its position at the margins.

Some would argue that adult education is now established and is no longer a marginal field of practice (Ilsley, 1992). Yet this chapter argues that adult education will never be mainstreamed, that we should embrace its position at the margins and use that position for social change. We agree with Sheared and Sissel (2001, p. 330) that "rather than spending time debating whether adult education is a legitimate discipline, we perhaps ought to revel in the fact that it is marginal; and more importantly, an alternative explanation for its marginalization in relation to the merging of these two words—*adult and education*—ought to be explored."

Adult Education as Social Action

Many authors (Collins, 1991; Ilsley, 1992; Cunningham, 1992) are concerned that adult education focuses too heavily on the individual's learning and should push for social justice and equality. Ilsley (1992, p. 33) writes:

> Adult education has tremendous drive, but no direction. . . . We do not have to be guided by the status quo. . . . Today social change commands attention. . . . It is to our advantage that adult education is a constantly moving, tension-filled and fluctuating field of practice, for this dynamism and flexibility enable us to discuss and respond to a myriad of social problems. But as long as we employ a content-centered approach to teaching adults, as if facts are neutral and values lie beyond our domain, the prominence of the values of the dominant culture is inevitable and implicit agreement with the vision of the status quo is maintained.

From its position at the margins, adult education has a great opportunity to work for change, both as an insider within organizations and as an outsider looking into issues with a critical and reflective eye (Hayes and Wilson, 2000). Much of the social research in adult education lately uses this position to speak about uses of power and politics as well as to add marginalized voices to the dialogue of education (Cervero and Wilson, 1994; Cervero, Wilson, and associates, 2001; Sheared and Sissel, 2001). "Every adult educator is a social activist regardless of his or her particular vision of society" (Cervero, Wilson, and associates, 2001, p. 13).

Most adult education happens beyond the view of traditional educational activities. Therefore, the forces at work to marginalize the field reflect forces in society. Apple (2001, p. ix) states that "our social system is crisscrossed by axes of class, gender, race, age, nationality, region, politics, religion, and other dynamics of power," creating a "complex nexus of power relations." Adult education sits in this mix as an ever present entity negotiating adult learning, but it seldom appears in the limelight.

Multiple Goals for Adult Education

Determining the numbers of adult educators is difficult, yet in his work "Future Directions for Adult and Continuing Education: A New Plateau," Knox (2004) found fifty "separate and robust national associations of people who work in the field" and that support "lifelong learning as central throughout society." He seeks to collaborate with these practitioners of adult education in other disciplines "to provide leadership in our provider agencies and in the field."

These practitioner areas embrace multiple perspectives and philosophies. Although it is difficult to identify a concrete and single direction, the diversity of populations served through collaborative relationships strengthen adult education research and practice. At times adult educators see commonalities across disciplines that others choose not to see. For example, leaders in human resource development choose to see their field as parallel to adult education, although adult education and human resource development leaders often use the same skill sets with differing guiding philosophies (Kuchinke, 1999). Cervero (1992, p. 48) reminds us "to recognize that different (and to some extent competing) purposes, knowledge and ideologies underlie the work of adult education"; however, "we must not trivialize the knowledge and practice of those who work outside the mainstream."

Each year business and industry, federal and state governments, and nonprofit and community groups spend billions of dollars on educating adults (U.S. Department of Education, 2004). Although each activity serves distinct audiences and purposes, all these programs share core adult education components.

Early on, Knowles (1962) recognized that adult educators needed to be connected to each other and other organizations. He described forces promoting coordination such as "overlapping markets of adult education services" and "the marginality of adult education in most institutional settings"; and he wrote that, "advances in knowledge and method occurring in one element of the field have implications for other elements" (p. 265). Yet Knowles was aware of the pressures on adult educators not to coordinate too much, such as "the lack of agreement on ultimate goals for adult education"; limits to "personal resources"; "differences in vocabularies, theoretical and philosophical positions, and differences in methodological approaches that interfere with communication"; and difficulty in "construct[ing] a coordinative organizational structure where the component parts of the field feel represented" (p. 266).

Even as the Future Directions project (Knox, 2004) seeks to link professional organizations, the field of adult education is becoming more divergent. Graduate programs often incorporate this diversity by collaborating with other departments to offer interdisciplinary degrees. One could take courses in departments such as human geography, philosophy, educational leadership, statistics, management, gerontology, sociology, curriculum and instruction, nursing, and women's studies. Heaney (2000, p. 561) explains that "individual practitioners do not define the field of adult education, nor do the experts. A definition of the field of practice is the social product of many individuals who negotiate the value and meaning of what they come to see as serving a common purpose over time."

As adult educators come to claim the position at the margins as their own, they will be in a better position to negotiate their work's values and meaning. Only by embracing the position at the margins can we shift the boundaries to value and include everyone's contribution: "We must go beyond the 'academy walls' in order to hear the voices of the other and make space for those in the margins, as well as in the center. It is this shifting of margins and centers that will allow for and create a new reality built on a foundation of inclusion of the multiple and varied realities of us all" (Sheared and Sissel, 2001, p. 330).

Embracing the Margins

How can adult education take advantage of and embrace its position at the margins? Adult education's position at the margins does not have to be detrimental. At times "marginality may render decision-making susceptible to external influences" (Clark, 1968, p. 149), yet working with stakeholders beyond its own control can be beneficial. Cervero and Wilson (1994, p. 4) understand that "adult educators are not free agents. . . . Rather their planning is always conducted within a complex set of personal, organizational, and social relationships of power among people who may have similar, different, or conflicting sets of interest."

The nature of lifelong learning, and of adult education itself, defines it as a collective activity, not a singular reality. Although adult educators may wish to create their own independent field of study, a number of groups share the underlying theories, methods, and philosophies for adult teaching and learning.

Adult educators revel in flexibility that allows them to adapt teaching and learning applications to the situation. However, Brockett (1989, p. 117) identified the primary challenge of adult education as "balancing unification and specialization," because without an awareness of the need for unification, adult education will "inevitably continue to suffer from fragmentation and lack of professional identity."

With diverse ideas and ideals, we develop allies but may struggle for a common direction. This also makes the voice of adult educators politically unheard by being so drowned out by multiple interests (Griffith, 1992).

Jarvis (1992), on the other hand, wishes to expand the scope of leadership in the field. "By having more leaders who are conversant with these debates, we can help make our field more mainstream. If leaders are drawn from the wider field, they would bring different perspectives and understandings that can only enrich our field" (p. 57).

Although marginality may be a "prime source of insecurity" (Clark, 1968, p. 149), it is also a position in which collaboration across groups is essential to promoting growth. Only by recognizing the power at the margins will adult educators be able to shift the debate and change the view from the center.

References

Apple, M. "Forward." In R. M. Cervero and A. L. Wilson (eds.), *Power in Practice: Adult Education and the Struggle for Knowledge and Power in Society.* San Francisco: Jossey-Bass, 2001.

Beder, H. "Purposes and Philosophies of Adult Education." In S. Merriam and P. Cunningham (eds.), *Handbook of Adult and Continuing Education.* San Francisco: Jossey-Bass, 1989.

Boshier, R. "A Conceptual Framework for Analyzing the Training of Trainers and Adult Educators." Reprinted in S. Brookfield (ed.), *Training Educators of Adults: The Theory and Practice of Graduate Adult Education.* Routledge: New York, 1988.

Brockett, R. G. "Professional Association for Adult and Continuing Education." In S. Merriam and P. Cunningham (eds.), *Handbook of Adult and Continuing Education.* San Francisco: Jossey-Bass, 1989.

Cervero, R. M. "Adult and Continuing Education Should Strive for Professionalization." In R. G. Brockett and M. W. Galbraith (eds.), *Confronting Controversies in Challenging Times: A Call for Action.* New Directions for Adult and Continuing Education, no. 54. San Francisco: Jossey-Bass, 1992.

Cervero, R. M., and Wilson, A. L. *Planning Responsibly for Adult Education: A Guide to Negotiating Power and Interests.* San Francisco: Jossey-Bass, 1994.

Cervero, R. M., Wilson, A. L., and associates. *Power in Practice: Adult Education and the Struggle for Knowledge and Power in Society.* San Francisco: Jossey-Bass, 2001.

Clark, B. *Adult Education in Transition: A Study of Institutional Insecurity.* Berkeley: University of California Press, 1968.

Collins, M. *Adult Education as Vocation: A Critical Role for the Adult Educator.* New York: Routledge, 1991.

Collins, M. "Adult and Continuing Education Should Resist Further Professionalization." In R. G. Brockett and M. W. Galbraith (eds.), *Confronting Controversies in Challenging Times: A Call for Action.* New Directions for Adult and Continuing Education, no. 54. San Francisco: Jossey-Bass, 1992.

Commission of Professors of Adult Education. "Standards for Graduate Programmes in Adult Education." Reprinted in S. Brookfield (ed.), *Training Educators of Adults: The Theory and Practice of Graduate Adult Education.* Routledge: New York, 1988.

Cunningham, P. "Adult and Continuing Education Does Not Need a Code of Ethics." In R. G. Brockett and M. W. Galbraith (eds.), *Confronting Controversies in Challenging Times: A Call for Action.* New Directions for Adult and Continuing Education, no. 54. San Francisco: Jossey-Bass, 1992.

Galbraith, M. W., and Gilley, J. W. "An Examination of Professional Certification." *Lifelong Learning,* 1985, 9(2), 12–15.

Griffith, W. S. "Has Adult and Continuing Education Fulfilled Its Early Promise?" In B. A. Quigley (ed.), *Fulfilling the Promise of Adult and Continuing Education.* New Directions for Continuing Education, no. 44. San Francisco: Jossey-Bass, 1992.

Hayes, E., and Wilson, A. (eds.). *Handbook of Adult and Continuing Education.* San Francisco: Jossey-Bass, 2000.

Heaney, T. W. "Adult Education and Society." In E. Hayes and A. Wilson (eds.), *Handbook of Adult and Continuing Education.* San Francisco: Jossey-Bass, 2000.

Houle, C. "The Development of Leadership." Chap. 4 in *Liberal Adult Education*. White Plains, N.Y.: Fund for Adult Education, 1956.

Ilsley, P. "The Undeniable Link: Adult and Continuing Education and Social Change." In R. G. Brockett and M. W. Galbraith (eds.), *Confronting Controversies in Challenging Times: A Call for Action*. New Directions for Adult and Continuing Education, no. 54. San Francisco: Jossey-Bass, 1992.

Imel, S., Brockett, R. G., and James, W. B. "Defining the Profession: A Critical Appraisal." In E. Hayes and A. Wilson (eds.), *Handbook of Adult and Continuing Education*. San Francisco: Jossey-Bass, 2000.

James, W. B. "Professional Certification Is Not Needed in Adult and Continuing Education." In R. G. Brockett and M. W. Galbraith (eds.), *Confronting Controversies in Challenging Times: A Call for Action*. New Directions for Adult and Continuing Education, no. 54. San Francisco: Jossey-Bass, 1992.

Jarvis, P. "Leaders of Adult and Continuing Education Should Come from Outside the Field." In R. G. Brockett and M. W. Galbraith (eds.), *Confronting Controversies in Challenging Times: A Call for Action*. New Directions for Adult and Continuing Education, no. 54. San Francisco: Jossey-Bass, 1992.

Knowles, M. S. *The Adult Education Movement in the United States*. Austin, Tex.: Holt, Rinehart and Winston, 1962.

Knowles, M. S. "A General Theory of the Doctorate in Education." Reprinted in S. Brookfield (ed.), *Training Educators of Adults: The Theory and Practice of Graduate Adult Education*. Routledge: New York, 1988.

Knox, A. B. *Strengthening Adult and Continuing Education: A Global Perspective on Synergistic Leadership*. San Francisco: Jossey-Bass, 1993.

Knox, A. B. "Future Directions for Adult and Continuing Education." AAACE-sponsored Web page. [http://www.aaace.org/futures/] (accessed Oct. 1, 2004).

Kuchinke, K. P. "Adult Development Towards What End? A Philosophical Analysis of the Concept as Reflected in the Research, Theory, and Practice of Human Resource Development." *Adult Education Quarterly,* 1999, *49*(4), 148–162.

Lindeman, E. *The Meaning of Adult Education*. Montreal, Quebec: Harvest House, 1926.

Merriam, S., and Cunningham, P. (eds.). *Handbook of Adult and Continuing Education*. San Francisco: Jossey-Bass, 1989.

Merriam, S. B., and Brockett, R. G. *The Profession and Practice of Adult Education: An Introduction*. San Francisco: Jossey-Bass, 1997.

Milton, J., Watkins, K. E., Studdard, S. S., and Burch, M. "The Ever Widening Gyre: Factors Affecting Change in Adult Education Graduate Programs in the United States." *Adult Education Quarterly,* 2003, *54*(1), 23–41.

Peterson's Graduate and Professional Programs: An Overview 2000. Lawrenceville, N.J.: Peterson's, 2000.

Sheared, V., and Sissel, P. A. (eds.). *Making Space: Merging Theory and Practice in Adult Education*. New York: Bergin & Garvey, 2001.

Sticht, T. G. "The Power of Adult Education: Moving the Adult Education and Literacy System of the United States from Margins to Mainstream of Education." Summary paper, California, January 2001. (ED 457410). [Available at http://www.nald.ca/fulltext/sticht/power/cover.htm.]

Stubblefield, H., and Keane, P. "The History of Adult and Continuing Education." In S. Merriam and P. Cunningham (eds.), *Handbook of Adult and Continuing Education*. San Francisco: Jossey-Bass, 1989.

U.S. Department of Education, National Center for Education Statistics. Chap. 4 in *Digest of Education Statistics:* "Table 369. U.S. Department of Education Appropriations for Major Programs, by State or Other Area: Fiscal Year 2001." [http://nces.ed.gov/programs/digest/d02/tables/dt369.asp] (accessed Oct. 5, 2004).

White, B. "Professional Certification Is a Needed Option for Adult and Continuing Education." In R. G. Brockett and M. W. Galbraith (eds.), *Confronting Controversies in*

Challenging Times: A Call for Action. New Directions for Adult and Continuing Education, no. 54. San Francisco: Jossey-Bass, 1992.

MICHELLE GLOWACKI-DUDKA *is an assistant professor of Adult, Higher, and Community Education at Ball State University.*

LORA B. HELVIE-MASON *is a doctoral student of Adult, Higher, and Community Education at Ball State University.*

2

*Collaboration across the domains of continuing educa-
tion and organizations advance civil society to address
public issues.*

From Margin to Mainstream to Collaboration: Regarding Public Issues

Alan B. Knox

Our current prospects regarding educational opportunities for adults reflect
both past trends and our future vision. This evolution is illustrated by this
chapter's focus on emerging trends in adult and continuing education on
behalf of democracy and public work.

The broad trend during the past century is inspiring. The proportion
of the adult population in North America that has participated in part-time
and short-term educational activities has increased each decade. This
reflects change and diversity that has stimulated adult participation and
helped expand the numbers and vitality of provider organizations with
their variety of program offerings (Kett, 1994; Stubblefield and Keane,
1994).

A review of adult education trends and prospects a half century ago
would likely have revealed marginality but also heartening expansion combined with high expectations for a field becoming more widespread, visible,
and beneficial. During the subsequent decades, some of us had high expectations for rising priority for educational opportunities that would enable
adults to experience productive and fulfilling lives and to help them create a
more humane and sustainable world (Blakely and Lappin, 1969; Knox, 2004).
I savor a conversation with Cy Houle fifty years ago when he said that what
he valued most about the field of adult education is what it could become.
Many current features exceed our wildest dreams. The field is certainly more
diverse and visible today, but the following rationale about using adult education to enhance democracy and attention to public issues highlights our
unmet challenge.

Creative Pioneers

There was much innovation within various types of educational programs for adults during the quarter century before the formation of the American Association for Adult Education (AAAE) in 1925 (Stubblefield and Keane, 1994). Social philosophy was a central theme of AAAE, which emphasized civic and cultural goals and through publications helped people associated with various marginal and invisible types of educational programs for adults to discover that they had much in common. The creation of the Adult Education Association at midcentury broadened the umbrella further and increased the potential for collaboration (Blakely and Lappin, 1969).

The trends in the field during the past half-century included increasing visibility, fragmentation, cost recovery, and occupational emphasis. Programs emphasizing citizenship and social change declined relative to rapid expansion of other segments that have not depended so heavily on subsidy. Admonitions urged balanced attention to various groups of adults, objectives, and methods (Knox, 1972). Most adult and continuing education programs have been at the margin of larger provider organizations that had other priorities that limited recognition and support but have allowed freedom for creative pioneers (Votruba, 1981).

In their book *Cultural Creatives,* Ray and Anderson (2000) chart the emergence of a segment of the adult population that has increased from 5 to 25 percent in the United States during the past forty years. Cultural creatives' characteristics, growth, and implications for personal and societal values have many parallels with adult and continuing education including lifestyles characterized by reading, discussion, and reflection in an active search for meaning, knowledge, and wisdom. Ray and Anderson (2000) contrast these values with the values of groups, which they characterize as traditionals (about one-quarter of the adult population) and as moderns (about one-half of the population).

A profound parallel between adult educators and cultural creatives generally is that in spite of diversity of their backgrounds and the specific causes and movements that inspire them, they are discovering that they are not alone. It is striking that issues related to personal potential and social progress are related; broadly shared values unite us and allow us to value diversity (Knox, 2002b). A special issue and a regular column on future directions in the journal *Adult Learning* reflect diverse perspectives on emerging trends.

Much of creativity occurs at the margins of science, the arts, and social policy. In adult education this evolution occurs at all levels: adult learners, educational activities, provider agencies, graduate study, and the adult and continuing education field in its societal context. Transitions from marginality to mainstream to collaboration reflect various influences, such as values, priorities, goals, and attention of a creative minority with a vision for change and the majority of people who are resistant to change (Musselwhite, 2003). Which is central and which is marginal?

Public Issues

Waning emphasis on adult education for adults' roles as citizens and focus on public responsibility has accompanied a long-term trend of increasing the extent, visibility, and vitality of the separate segments (types of organizations) that provide adult education, such as community colleges and social organizations. There are several influences on this paradoxical trend. Extensive social change and diversity can stimulate a quest for meaning and lifelong learning (Kane, 1996). All types of institutions and organizations provide educational opportunities for adults that in part reflect their mission and expectations regarding return on investment.

Increasing numbers of practitioners are familiar with concepts about adults as learners, about program development and coordination, and about trends and issues in the field. In spite of this, the field has been expanding even more rapidly. Also, most practitioners are part-time and emphasize procedures instead of goals and priorities. Urbanization, a shift from grassroots democracy to representative government, and polarizing mass media have discouraged educational activity regarding public issues. This places a high premium on a relatively small creative minority of people with vision and commitment toward adult education for public responsibility.

Fortunately, assistance is available from other people who recognize the growing importance of public work for a personal search for meaning and for a humane and democratic society (Boyte, 2004; Boyte and Kari, 1996). Typically, the impetus is from trying to resolve public issues related to community, work, family, religious congregation, or health. A related local goal is to democratize power relations as adults engage in community or organization development as a part of their paid and volunteer work, thus pursuing public work. Civic journalism can also help people progress beyond either-or Manichean polarization through deliberation, negotiation, and problem solving related to public issues. Adult and continuing education activities regarding public responsibility can help diverse people understand broad interdependence. Collaboration among cultural creatives, people facilitating public work, and various providers of educational opportunities for adults can constitute a critical mass sufficient for progress on public issues.

Collaborative Strategies

Why bother with a joint program on public responsibility when it seems easier to do so independently? Some providers do. Examples of collaboration include those characterized by community development, discussion and action regarding public issues, and some faith-based organizations concerned with social justice (Wood, 2002). Following is a basic rationale for local collaboration.

Some topics are important enough to warrant concerted effort even though individual provider agencies give them low priority. Especially since September 11, 2001, reversing neglected attention to adult education for public responsibility and citizen role has gained renewed importance. Beyond our general commitment to providing opportunities for adults to pursue an active search for meaning on topics of their choice, we have a professional obligation to help them transcend simplistic either-or thinking about public work and value issues by progressing to higher levels of understanding. This entails reflection, interpretation, compassion, enlightenment, wisdom, and unity.

With a focus on local democracy, it is desirable to serve a broad cross section of adults. This entails addressing the gap between haves and have-nots to achieve greater equality and democracy. Unfortunately, adult education is voluntary and mainly attracts people who are ready to participate. Thus, we inadvertently help widen the gap because higher proportions of adults with increasing levels of education participate. Different providers vary in the characteristics of adults whom they attract and serve. In the aggregate the total field touches the entire adult population. Collaborative programs enable us to bring together participants with diverse viewpoints and backgrounds to explore public dimensions of their roles in work, family, and community that entail attention to values, power, justice, negotiation, and wisdom.

Collaboration also helps reduce risks to cooperating providers. Educational programs on community issues and public work are unlikely to recover costs from participant fees, so cosponsors can share the subsidy. Analysis of public issues can be controversial, so collaboration can help assure evenhandedness in a search for shared values, in which the process of inquiry, negotiation, and appreciation of diverse viewpoints is one important aim.

Much of political debate, demonstrations, and mass media attention oversimplifies and polarizes important and admittedly complex public issues. This, combined with growing distrust of institutions and declines in adult face-to-face engagement regarding public issues in community organizations, presents a crucial challenge to adult and continuing education. We can collaboratively provide mediating forums for deliberation, negotiation, and problem solving related to local, national, and international public issues that can help diverse people recognize broad interdependence and gain wisdom regarding their common destiny.

Successful collaboration requires shared leadership. A starting point is recognition that each local program on public responsibility has its own history, context, purposes, arrangements, and types of learning activities. Similarly, each partner has its own mission, culture, and expectations regarding contributions and benefits. Effective leadership entails articulating a pervasive rationale regarding program purposes, procedures, and benefits. Sustained collaborative leadership depends on partners willing and able to work together in pursuit of a shared vision and mutually beneficial exchanges, even as they negotiate differences. Ongoing evaluation can contribute to program planning, improvement, and assessment of results (Knox, 2002a).

Illustrative Approaches

During 2003 people associated with ten distinctive exemplary educational opportunities for adults on public issues agreed to exchange program information. The following brief summaries reflect program development strategies that five of them used over several years. The overview and updates for all ten projects, prepared by this author and project coordinator, are available from the following Web site: http://www.soemadison.wisc.edu/edadmin/people/faculty/knox/futures.htm.

Citizen Leadership Institute (CLI), Gulf Coast Community College (GCCC), Florida. CLI has contributed to the GCCC's distinctive evolution of its continuing education and lifelong learning mission. With the focus on collaborative community problem solving, the CLI mission of GCCC has multiple contributors and beneficiaries, including faculty members, students, and local citizens.

Through programs such as the Sun-Up Seminars that engage students with faculty and community, Great Decisions local forums, Public Policy Institutes, and state and national award-winning Citizen Leadership Training Program, the GCCC has persisted in its mission to advance democratic principles and cultivate citizen leaders. Examples of the widespread public issues that GCCC's lifelong learning function addresses include growth management, environmental protection, workforce development, poverty, crime, illiteracy, health, and family relations.

A renewed GCCC commitment to civic engagement has reoriented CLI in a new direction. Assembling diverse participants to discuss public issues is essential to the CLI goal and rationale. CLI involves stakeholders in framing issues for community forums in order to achieve diversity and a broader reach into the community. For example, the GCCC staff has been very active in the Community College National Center for Community Engagement that is currently providing training in five sites. In February 2004 a summit on homeland security presented ways in which higher education institutions can increase attention to security and overall emergency preparedness within their organization and in their service area.

GCCC collaborates with the two other community colleges to provide leadership for the Community College National Center for Community Engagement to provide training for civic engagement and service learning at five sites nationally. Other partners for CLI generally include the League for Innovation, the National Council for Continuing Education and Training, the American Association of Community Colleges, and the Kettering Foundation.

The continuing education dean and GCCC president have involved multiple stakeholders in leadership on behalf of CLI. Funding for CLI is decentralized and comes from various sources, typically in small amounts. Aspirations for all that could be accomplished with limited resources have left little time or money for evaluation. However, the dean and others recognize the potential of evaluation to strengthen CLI. Researchers developed and used an evaluation model for CLI's initial project with the W. K. Kellogg Foundation to assess impact of the CLI's Citizen Leadership Training Program. Given limited resources, however, these initial evaluation efforts have not been sustained. For a full overview see http://www.soemadison.wisc.edu/edadmin/people/faculty/knox/futures.htm, item AM.

Council for Public Deliberation (CPD), Ohio. CPD is a community group dedicated to promoting deliberative democracy by engaging citizens in discussions of issues important to the local community and the nation. The council accomplishes its mission by sponsoring deliberative forums, providing training for citizen moderators, and partnering with local organizations to conduct discussion groups.

In October 2002 the National Issues Forum and the Kettering Foundation announced a new issue book and discussion guide titled *America's Role in the World.* A national campaign with media involvement sponsored by MacNeil/Lehrer Productions included grants to local PBS stations. During the spring of 2003, the Council for Public Deliberation, Columbus, in partnership with the Ohio State University Civic Life Institute, the Catholic Diocese of Columbus, the Columbus Metropolitan Library, the Columbus Council on World Affairs, the Ohio Humanities Council, and other community and religious organizations organized community forums.

Between mid-April and mid-May 2003, over 160 central Ohio residents attended one of six public forums in cosponsors' facilities to discuss the United States's role in the world. Cooperation from many community organizations yielded volunteers and helped attract participants, but each cooperating organization attracted participants who were predictably similar to each other.

Based on earlier CPD attempts to conduct forums alone and on its success in cosponsorship, CPD favors a collaborative approach in the future. Because the local PBS station (WOSU) did not receive a grant, it, CPD, and cooperating organizations shared the costs largely by in-kind contributions. Local conveners contributed publicity, refreshments, and facilities. WOSU provided spot announcements.

A report based on a postforum questionnaire and summaries by recorders and observers at each forum indicated the participants' sentiments about the four broad approaches presented in the National Issues Forum issue book and discussion guide. More attention to evaluation is desirable. For a full overview see http://www.soemadison.wisc.edu/edadmin/people/faculty/knox/futures.htm, item AH.

Restorative Justice, Madison-Area Urban Ministry (MUM), Wisconsin. The Restorative Justice project is a major activity of MUM, an interfaith justice organization that links over one hundred congregations in aspects of its work. During its history MUM conceived and hatched fourteen of the most innovative and community-building nonprofits in the area.

Restorative Justice addresses the transition of prisoners who will be rejoining the wider community. It includes viewing of a film, a simulation, support circles, and other activities. Two-thirds of Wisconsin prison admissions are due to revocations of probation or parole. The project intends to reduce that cycle of recidivism. This would better the community and would turn around those who are now on that destructive path.

Following are four major components of the Restorative Justice project.

- *Documentary film.* Speaker teams show the film Today's Prisoners, Tomorrow's Neighbors to about forty-five or more groups a year. A MUM staff member and a former prisoner (who is a member of the Voices Beyond Bars speakers' bureau) share life stories and answer questions. At least five hundred people view the film and take part in the discussion per year.
- *Returning prisoner simulation.* In these intense simulations, participants try to accomplish tasks such as they would during the first four weeks after release from incarceration. Adults and teenagers come together, share a meal, and walk in a parolee's shoes.
- *Circles of support.* After the previous steps, people volunteer to work with former prisoners in a support group. MUM trains, matches, and coordinates these circles of support, made up of four or five volunteers who meet regularly with a newly released former prisoner for at least six months as they negotiate the journey of returning to life in the community.
- *Voices Beyond Bars.* This speakers' bureau develops the leadership skills, mutual support, and personal and public responsibility of at least twenty former prisoners.

In fall 2003 a very successful prisoner simulation included corrections staff as participants. This led to a new collaboration with correctional institutions in which MUM is scheduling simulations for corrections staff.

Staff recruitment, orientation, and assistance to volunteers regarding core teams and circles of support entails ongoing collaboration. MUM staff and volunteers have provided leadership for Restorative Justice activities by working with faith communities on social action, gaining support for a shared vision, developing materials, and collaborating with related stakeholders to make progress.

Each year the program serves about fifteen hundred participants or assisted persons. Several dozen volunteers are oriented, and then each one provides about ten hours of service each month. Program evaluations at six and twelve months indicate benefits. Staff is interested in more detailed pro-

gram evaluation. For a full overview see http://www.soemadison.wisc.edu/
edadmin/people/faculty/knox/futures.htm, item AJ.

Third Age Initiative, Leadership Greater Hartford, Connecticut.
Leadership Greater Hartford serves community-minded leaders who address
key issues facing Greater Hartford. Third Age Initiative is the agency's year-
long program for seniors who want to develop their leadership to give back
to the community.

The project's goals and objectives include

- Establishing a training program for dozens of community elders per year
- Increasing the number of senior citizens active in serving the Greater
  Hartford community
- Informing participants of the challenges, assets, and opportunities for
  community leadership
- Enhancing participants' capacities to be effective community leaders
- Developing projects for community leaders and organizations
- Inspiring participants to serve the community and to help with new efforts
- Becoming a model program for dissemination and replication

Each year older adults interested in an issue, such as the impact of
poverty on children, housing, food, or literacy, form participant teams. Many
volunteers are interested in providing leadership for team projects.

The fifth class enrolled twenty-nine participants, which brings the total
between 2001 and 2004 to 134 people aged from forty-eight to eighty-eight.
Team projects have been varied, including work on issues such as restorative justice, family life, neighborhood parks, voter turnout, oral history, and
mentoring of children. A project goal is diversity of participants and project
clients. An early activity for each class is a community sampler tour that
provides participants an overview and allows them to select projects.

Funding is an ongoing challenge as the initial subsidy is replaced by
participant fees. Scholarships are provided for about 20 percent of each class
classified as low income. Teams have raised funds to continue to support
ongoing projects for schools or parks.

One challenge is matching team preferences regarding their contribution to organizational expectations. Program benefits include participant
growth and contributions, community problem solving, enhanced capacity
of project clients, and ongoing civic engagement of program graduates. Half
of team projects continue beyond the project year. Eighty-five percent of the
graduates from the first two classes reported that they took on new community leadership responsibilities with additional projects. Program evaluation has included several procedures, including formation of an evaluation
committee, participant self-assessments, personal written comments,
observers for group sessions, phone interviews, and team debriefings. For
a full overview see http://www.soemadison.wisc.edu/edadmin/people/faculty/
knox/futures.htm, item AI.

Neighborhood Learning Community (NLC), Jane Addams School for Democracy, Minnesota. NLC is a collaborative, intergenerational project located on the low-income West Side of St. Paul, which has a high proportion of Latino and Hmong residents. NLC has multiple stakeholders and organizational partners.

NLC's broad purpose and vision is to improve learning for children and families on the West Side. The project emerges from the Jane Addams School for Democracy (JAS), a community-based education and social action initiative. The JAS mission is to improve literacy and civic capacity. A seven-year experiment in community-based learning, JAS has acted as catalyst and resource to other organizations and residents for a variety of neighborhood and regional public work initiatives. Residents of the West Side and participants of the JAS created the NLC concept.

The West Side neighborhood, a portal for immigrants dating back to the midnineteenth century, is in many ways an ideal setting for this project. The total NLC initiative focuses on public work, democracy, and empowerment in St. Paul's West Side neighborhood; only part of the initiative focuses on the education of adults regarding public issues. Examples of educational opportunities provided by JAS that met for multiple sessions were the Hmong adult circle (170 participants) and the Spanish-speaking circle (forty-eight participants).

Approximately 250 adults of many ages participate. Three-quarters are women, and about one-third live in the neighborhood. With the JAS emphasis on valuing diversity so that participants learn to negotiate different interests and perspectives, it is reassuring that they embrace the belief that everyone is both a teacher and a learner.

Program staff identified both negative and positive influences on educational progress. Negative influences included poverty, cultural barriers, racism, lack of institutional collaboration, and professional practices that disempowered people rather than building capacity. Positive influences related to educational activities such as one-on-one tutoring; intergenerational learning activities; connections between education and community, including formal and informal opportunities; and praxis between learning and action.

Since JAS began in 1996, it and NLC have expanded greatly. For example, the numbers of cooperating organizations increased from four in 2001 to thirty in 2003. Along with many informal types of capacity building and leadership development, by the fall of 2003, on most evenings about two hundred people participated in learning circles and other activities on topics such as literacy, citizenship, parenting, language, culture, and leadership.

A research firm and a university center have provided ongoing evaluation to identify trends, influences, and outcomes related to the NLC effort.

The foregoing five examples illustrate some widespread themes for collaborative leadership regarding public issues. Leadership entailed achieving a shared vision of desirable future directions. Because most major societal issues are complex, it was important that the adult education activity had a manageable focus. Collaborative program development strategies increased the diversity of participants, which was important for goal achievement, as well as for attracting volunteers, in-kind contributions, and external grants that helped to address the problems, restraints, and challenges associated with insufficient resources. The staff was committed to increasing the inadequate program evaluation needed to strengthen planning, improvement, and support. These and other exemplars reflect desirable directions for adult and continuing education on public issues. For a full overview see http://www.soemadison.wisc.edu/edadmin/people/faculty/knox/futures.htm, item AO.

Leadership Implications

Support for collaborative programs on public issues depends on a compelling rationale for their desirability and feasibility. People who seek to encourage a shared vision about the importance of such programs and contributions toward achievement of public work goals should address at least three constituencies: scholars, local providers, and national associations. Ongoing evaluation (action research) can be a valuable resource for program planning, improvement, and accountability (Knox, 2002a).

The rationale in this chapter can be summarized as follows. Current widespread concern about local, national, and international issues warrants concerted efforts by adult and continuing education providers. Such educational efforts can complement various forms of mobilization and protest that public issues generate, and they can help offset the extreme simplification and polarization to which politicians and media contribute.

Collaborative educational programs can serve as common ground for adults with diverse viewpoints to explore controversial public issues and thereby can strengthen participatory democracy (Boyte, 2004; Skocpol, 2003). A focus on public work in family, occupation, and community includes connections between personal and community life. Illustrative topics include healthy lifestyles, ecologically sound practices, restorative justice, parenting guidelines, community problem solving, and constructive foreign policy. The educational process should emphasize ingredients of local democracy such as reflection, compassion, diversity, negotiation, wisdom, and application.

For about seventy years, scholars have been the main source of a fieldwide vision of educational opportunities for adults. The leadership of AAAE was made up mainly of social philosophers committed to the concept of lifelong learning. The creation of graduate programs to study adult education resulted in professors, students, and research that spanned the field. Dissertations have constituted a major portion of the research base. Professors and their students and alumni have been prominent in fieldwide associations (such as the American Association for Adult and Continuing Education, or AAACE) and research conferences, have authored and edited books and journals, won awards for excellence, and won election to the Hall of

Fame. Thus, having the support of scholars and scholarly practitioners is important for the success of a collaborative effort regarding public responsibility (Knox, 2004).

The essence of adult education for public responsibility is local. National efforts serve to strengthen local collaborative programs, but the mutually beneficial exchange among local providers is crucial for initiating and sustaining successful collaborative programs. Mutual respect and complementary contributions enhance success. Each cooperating provider typically brings valuable resources and a distinctive clientele, which adds to diverse viewpoints that are important for strengthening the process of local democracy. In addition to increasing their understanding of public issues, participants who explore and negotiate diverse viewpoints are empowered to participate effectively in community problem solving.

Local adult and continuing education providers vary greatly in the extent of their collaboration with other providers, which might enhance some aspects of their mission. Most local providers are connected with at least one of more than fifty specialized national associations that serve their segment of the field. The distinctive mission of AAACE is its field-wide scope that can enhance solidarity, visibility, and impact. However, many of the specialized associations recognize the importance of working together on matters of mutual interest, such as leadership, advocacy, standards, visibility, and joint meetings and publications. A compelling collaborative vision and procedures for cooperation can strengthen alliances for advancement of the field (Blakely and Lappin, 1969). Dozens of items on future directions are available from the AAACE futures Web page (http://www.aaace.org/futures).

The importance of initiating and strengthening collaborative programs on public issues warrants attention to reflection and evaluation. We are more likely to be reflective in our planning, implementation, and accountability if there is ongoing evaluation. Action research is an especially appropriate form of evaluation for this purpose (Quigley and Kuhne, 1997). Partners help design the evaluative feedback to guide responsive planning, continuous improvement, and reporting to major stakeholders about outcomes. Fortunately, there are resources to guide such evaluation throughout (Knox, 2002a). The importance of goals related to public issues and the dance of successful collaborations justify sound evaluation.

References

Blakely, R. J., and Lappin, I. M. *Knowledge Is Power to Control Power: New Institutional Arrangements and Organizational Patterns for Continuing Education.* Syracuse, N.Y.: Syracuse University Publications in Continuing Education, 1969.

Boyte, H. C. *Everyday Politics: Repairing Democracy's Roots.* Philadelphia: University of Pennsylvania Press, 2004.

Boyte, H. C., and Kari, N. *Building America.* Philadelphia: Temple University Press, 1996.

Kane, R. *Through the Moral Maze.* Armonk, N.Y.: Sharpe, 1996.

Kett, J. F. *The Pursuit of Knowledge Under Difficulties: From Self-Improvement to Adult Education in America, 1750–1990.* Stanford, Calif.: Stanford University Press, 1994.

Knox, A. B. "Achieving the Fifth Freedom." *Adult Leadership,* 1972, *21*(3), 100–104.

Knox, A. B. *Evaluation for Continuing Education: A Comprehensive Guide to Success.* San Francisco: Jossey-Bass, 2002a.

Knox, A. B. "A Shared Vision for Adult and Continuing Education." *Adult Education Quarterly,* 2002b, *52*(4), 328–333.

Knox, A. B. (ed.). "Future Directions." *Adult Learning,* 2004, *13*(4) (special issue).

Musselwhite, C. "Managing Change." In M. J. Johnson, D. E. Hanna, and D. Olcott (eds.), *Bridging the Gap.* Madison, Wis.: Atwood, 2003.

Quigley, B. A., and Kuhne, G. W. (eds.). *Creating Practical Knowledge Through Action Research.* New Directions for Adult and Continuing Education, no. 73. San Francisco: Jossey-Bass, 1997.

Ray, P. H., and Anderson, S. R. *Cultural Creatives.* New York: Three Rivers Press, 2000.

Skocpol, T. *Diminished Democracy.* Norman: University of Oklahoma Press, 2003.

Stubblefield, H. W., and Keane, P. *Adult Education in the American Experience.* San Francisco: Jossey-Bass, 1994.

Votruba, J. D. (ed.). *Strengthening Internal Support for Continuing Education.* New Directions for Continuing Education, no. 9. San Francisco: Jossey-Bass, 1981.

Wood, R. L. *Faith in Action: Religion, Race, and Democratic Organizing in America.* Chicago: University of Chicago Press, 2002.

ALAN B. KNOX *is professor of Educational Leadership and Policy Analysis at the University of Wisconsin–Madison and chairs the Futures Project for the American Association for Adult and Continuing Education.*

3

*Two adult and religious educators—a Muslim and a
Jew—demonstrate the impact of interreligious dialogue
on personal transformation and democratic social change.*

Crossing Borders of Religious Difference: Adult Learning in the Context of Interreligious Dialogue

Nadira K. Charaniya, Jane West Walsh

Interreligious dialogue experiences throughout the last century have primarily been projects directed by individuals and religious groups with a vision for fostering greater tolerance and harmony in the world. Religious institutional leaders or scholars of religion have generally organized them for intellectually curious congregants and students, often as a way to foster understanding and political harmony between religious groups at the leadership or congregational levels. Scholars who studied and reflected on these projects were primarily working in the academic disciplines of religion (for example, Harvard University's Pluralism Project) and, to a lesser extent, religious education (Boys and Lee, 1996).

They have not been situated—either as a methodology or as a particular context for learning—in the field of adult and continuing education. It is true that some contexts and movements fall squarely within the field in which interreligious dialogue may have taken place (for example, with the civil rights and peace movements or at places such as Highlander Folk School). However, even in these contexts, whatever dialogue may have existed has been incidental. The field of adult education does include scholarship in the area of adult religious education (Elias, 1993) as well as scholarship relating to learning across borders of difference (Guy, 1999; Hayes and Colin, 1994; Hayes and Flannery, 2000; Hill, 1995; Johnson-Bailey and Cervero, 2000; Sheared and Sissel, 2001; Tisdell, 1995, 1998, 1999) and the role of spirituality in adult education (Dirkx, 1997; English and

New Directions for Adult and Continuing Education, no. 104, Winter 2004 © Wiley Periodicals, Inc.

Gillen, 2000; Tisdell, 2003). However, little scholarship in the field specifically explores the crossing of borders of religious difference.

The literature does not address interreligious dialogue as a learning experience that can be systematically directed, planned for, or researched. It does not explore the nature of the learning that occurs within an interreligious experience when individuals cross into a different religious context, nor does it explore how such experiences reshape their understanding of the world. The only literature that we have come across in the field that relates to this area of adult education is our own doctoral work and the conference papers that emerged from that process (Charaniya and Walsh, 2001a, 2001b, 2001c; Walsh and Charaniya, 2000).

With the events of September 11, 2001, the dialogue of religious difference has been thrust into the public discourse as central to fostering democratic civil society and social change. We believe that interreligious learning is an ever more crucial focus for the emerging border-crossing inquiry within adult education, with the borders defined by religious self-understanding and the resulting sense of belonging derived from participating in a community of shared religious commitment. In this chapter we provide examples from our research—as two adult and religious educators, a Muslim and a Jew—that demonstrate the impact of interreligious dialogue on personal transformation and democratic social change.

Our Story

We are a Muslim and a Jew, both religious and adult educators, who were engaged in adult education doctoral studies at National-Louis University in Chicago between 1998 and 2001. In the context of the intensive learning community of a doctoral cohort, we became interested in learning from one another about our different religious traditions and the way they are taught in the context of U.S. society. Through this ongoing interreligious dialogue, at first incidentally, then consciously and purposefully, we gained new knowledge about Islam and Judaism and the teaching and learning that takes place within our religious communities. These experiences, and the work of Boys and Lee (1996), inspired us to conduct a research project to learn more about how adults who belong to different religious traditions learn from one another about one another (Charaniya and Walsh, 2001a).

Jane is a third-generation Jewish American woman who grew up in a small city in eastern Pennsylvania in the 1950s and 1960s. Three of her grandparents immigrated to Philadelphia from Poland and Russia in the early twentieth century. She has worked actively as a professional Jewish educator since 1981, engaged in developing and facilitating teaching and learning programs for Jews of all ages, in communities across the United States and in Jerusalem, Israel. Her exposure to Islam and Muslims (prior to her meeting Nadira) was limited to academic coursework and books, participation as a guest in Iftar meals (served at the end of the day during

Ramadan, to break the day's fast), film, and media reports. While living and studying in Israel, she had an opportunity to visit the Islamic Museum and the Al Aqsa mosque and met and spoke with a few Muslim Palestinians in Jerusalem. With these relatively limited experiences, her assumptions about Muslims were limited, based on a relatively monolithic understanding of Islam. It was an understanding that was primarily filtered through the face of the Muslim communities of the Middle East, with some additional awareness of the uniquely U.S. bent of the followers of the Nation of Islam.

Nadira is a Shia Ismaili Muslim of East Indian ancestry, born in Zaire. She has lived in seven different cities, in four countries, on three continents. She has been an assistant professor, religious educator, adjunct instructor, and educational consultant. Her exposure to Judaism and Jews (prior to her encounter with Jane) was limited. It was primarily based on media coverage of the Israeli-Palestinian situation, textbook encounters through formal education, relationships with secular Jews, historical accounts of Muslim-Jewish encounters, and Qur'anic literature on the relationship of Muslims and Jews (as well as Christians) as having originated from Abraham. Her assumptions about Jews were based on an understanding of Judaism as a monolithic body of religious tradition and practice.

The Inquiry

Our collaborative research gave us a glimpse into the nature of the learning and impact of interreligious dialogue on adult learners. Our two-and-a-half-year qualitative research study investigated the nature of the learning in four separate contexts: (1) our own experiences of learning from one another in dialogue as a Muslim and a Jew, (2) a dialogue group of parallel Jewish and Muslim neighboring religious communities responding to a crisis (the Shalom-Salaam group), (3) a communitywide Christian-Jewish dialogue program, and (4) a Christian-Jewish women's dialogue group. Here we will share details from the first two contexts.

Researcher Dialogue

Our dialogue, which began as an academic and intellectually stimulating exercise, resulted in personal expressions of social action. From our initial encounters as fellow students involved in a cohort-based doctoral program eventually emerged a conversation about our surprisingly common goals as U.S. religious and adult educators and our mutually held conviction that greater understanding was needed between people who are committed to different religious traditions and worldviews. Our own interreligious dialogue and learning and its impact in helping both of us better understand each other led us to think about how the vehicle of interreligious dialogue as a context for adult learning might be having an impact on others, particularly in moving participants toward envisioning and creating a better world. We asked ourselves: What would it look like if the social spaces North Americans share were filled with sincere dialogue about our ideas and assumptions, our definitions and our feelings about our religious commitments and how they impact our everyday decisions and actions? What would it look like when adults learned how to cross borders of religious difference through dialogue, without becoming assimilated into what lies on the other side (Charaniya and Walsh, 2001a)?

Our growing interest in each other as religious people, combined with the encouraging environment of the doctoral program at National-Louis University, sparked our research project together; but our research and growing awareness of the potential power of interreligious dialogue ultimately transformed us as adults engaged in the larger issues that challenge civil society. Jane captured some of the impact of this when she wrote

> As I have come to know Nadira, and how she lives her life, and the other Muslims that I have met in my research and life here in (Illinois), I cannot but think that Islam and Judaism have a great deal to share, and that the golden age in Spain must have been a glorious time of learning and sharing in deep and powerful ways, . . . now I understand it in a more tacit and personal way. It gives me the glimpse of hope I need, as we strive to make peace more prominent than hatred, everywhere we live. Our work is focused on America and not Israel, but we are both convinced that our efforts here to understand and foster adult learning in the context of interreligious dialogue do make a difference. I feel that each word we write together is like a prayer for peace that we both hold dear in our hearts (Charaniya and Walsh, 2001a).

Eck (1993, p. 219) tells us "People of every religious tradition depend upon one another to interpret one another fairly and accurately. We are the keepers of one another's image." One very poignant example of how participation in interreligious dialogue has engendered this attitude of keepers of another's image is the response by Nadira's circle of interreligious dialogue partners and colleagues to the nightmare ordeal she encountered in the wake of the September 11 attacks and the corresponding strategy of national security. She was one of the victims of our government's early zeal to isolate potential terrorists and blame someone.

Having been contacted by the U.S. Customs Service, acting under the auspices of the Department of Homeland Security, regarding allegations that she was supporting terrorist activities, Nadira turned to Jane for comfort and solace. Jane's actions in response to what had happened can only be described as social action at its best. Within a matter of days, Jane had contacted the investigating customs agent, found out the mailing address to write on Nadira's behalf, and managed to rally about forty of the Christian and Jewish acquaintances with whom they had met during work together. The strategy to fill the homeland security file with evidence of Nadira's commitment to U.S. democratic ideals, by writing letters in which descriptions of Nadira's behavior and the projects in which she was involved, would loudly and articulately communicate her passion to the very work of fostering democratic interreligious understanding and cooperation. Not only did the response of Jane and the other friends and colleagues provide solid, concrete evidence of the action that can emerge out of the interreligious dialogue process, it enabled Nadira to truly feel a part of civil society at a time when it would have been easier for her to have simply felt disdain and horror at that society.

Shalom-Salaam Group

Another example of the potential and power of interreligious dialogue for personal transformation and democratic social change is the Shalom-Salaam group. This Muslim-Jewish dialogue group began as a social action project in which several individuals responded to incidents of hostility and xenophobia within one suburban community where a mosque and Islamic educational center were to be built. A local Muslim community had developed detailed plans to build a mosque and educational center and, because of the size and location, a zoning hearing was required. Neighbors in the surrounding community, some of whom were Jews, voiced a lot of opposition to this proposed project. Responding to the resulting animosity and misunderstanding, some Jews and Muslims got together to imagine a different future through learning about each other and from each other.

Reshma, a Muslim participant in this group, shared with us her encounter with an elderly Jewish woman at a public meeting about the proposed mosque, which took place years before September 11, 2001:

> There was such animosity against the Muslims, and I have come from a background where everybody was a Muslim so for me I never thought of myself being anything abnormal or unusual. I was a Muslim, and if you were not a Muslim, that was no problem for me, but apparently it was a problem for this group of people. There was this one lady, and this was like six or seven years ago, and I still distinctly remember. . . . She was sitting across the room. It was a big room, with a lot of people, and this was an old woman. And she looked at me in the eye and she said, "I don't want you making bombs in my back yard." And it took my breath away, and I didn't realize that—is this what people think a Muslim would be? I never thought of myself as a bomb maker or a terrorist or somebody who doesn't follow the law, and it took me aback, and I was very offended. And actually I said, "Oh, well, I don't really care what you think," but I really did care. I didn't want her to think that that's all Muslims are about. And then this dialogue was born out of that (Charaniya and Walsh, 2001a).

She went on to tell us that growing up in Pakistan, practically everyone that she met was a Muslim. Although she had been living in the United

States for over ten years when this incident with the mosque happened, she shared with us how she understood that her thinking had changed: "I never, until this thing happened, never really gave any serious thought to anybody's religion. I thought your religion is your business, and it has nothing to do with me as an individual. And then I realized that that perhaps was not true and that what you do as an individual has a lot to do with your religious perspective or how you think of yourself in the environment" (Charaniya and Walsh, 2001a).

Shalom-Salaam participants today, several years after the crisis surrounding the mosque ended and the mosque and educational center were built, are an informal extension of the original group who met in response to that crisis. This particular group has remained in touch and connected for over nine years and continues to meet several times each year, to learn about each other from each other. Not only does this group continue to meet and learn about each other, members of the group also engage in various social action projects together—from letter-writing campaigns to educational endeavors in public settings. It is notable that they continue to meet even after the tragic circumstances of September 11, 2001, have challenged other dialogue groups in ways that caused them to discontinue.

Discussion

Both of these cases demonstrate how engaging in interreligious dialogue can be transformative. Both Kegan (2000) and Daloz (2000) tell us that transformative experiences are those that change one's very frame of reference. Daloz (p. 104) writes: "What shifts in the transformative process is our very epistemology—the way in which we know and make meaning." Interreligious dialogue and the learning that emerges from that process is transformative in this sense.

The transformation that can occur as a result of participation in interreligious dialogue can be seen in three possible forms: transformed worldviews, new behaviors, and/or fresh visions of how interreligious dialogue can change society. A profound aspect of these changes is an embodiment of the perspective that one has "to *participate* in pluralism. [We] can't just stand by and watch" (Eck, 1993, p. 191).

Interreligious dialogue participants in our study have reported a change in their attitudes about, and outlook toward, both self and other. It is an acknowledgment of what Jean Halpering, a Jewish scholar, means when saying, "We not only need to understand one another, we need one another to understand ourselves" (cited in Eck, 1993, p. 189). That is, how one views one's own religious tradition and the symbols within it have a profound impact on one's stance toward the other. This change in worldview is especially important for those individuals with educational roles in their religious communities, because such roles in a democratic society pose the challenge of educating for the particular without negating the pluralistic.

A second impact of transformation resulting from participation in interreligious dialogue is the change in behaviors that result from a new understanding of self and other. These behaviors appear to change when individuals are presented with Daloz's fourth condition of transformation (2000): opportunity for committed action. (The other three include the presence of the other, reflective discourse, and a mentoring community.) It is not that people necessarily have to go out of their way to change the world; but when the opportunity presents itself, they eagerly move forward. Whether subtle or overt, all such change in behavior results from changed understandings and attitudes experienced in the context of interreligious dialogue with the other. The examples of the actions that members of the Shalom-Salaam group took and the response to Nadira's post-September 11 ordeal are testimony to this.

Social Action

Other aspects of social action resulting from participation in interreligious dialogue include the following: (1) voluntary participation in committees that consider interreligious issues within the institutional structure of one's own religious group; (2) increased ability to represent the complexities of the other religion in contrast to one's own, in social or educational contexts; (3) increased deliberation and critical reflection before emotionally responding to media reports of incidents involving the interaction of members of the two religious groups; (4) voluntary engagement in self-directed learning projects such as independent reading, learning from others not in the dialogue program (through conversation about their religious ideas and practices), watching videos or films, and enrollment in formal courses and programs of study of religion; (5) articulation of hope for further opportunities for action; and (6) articulation of a positive vision of a better future for the world and the next generation, as a result of the learning and modeling for others.

The optimism with which one envisions the impact of interreligious dialogue on society profoundly affects the manner in which one envisages the world and is one of the ways in which interreligious dialogue can lead to transformation. For those individuals for whom interreligious dialogue is itself a form of social action, the task is to learn about and understand the other on the other's terms so that we are better able to keep this "sacred trust" (Eck, 1993, p. 219). It is recognition that "No religion is an island" and that "We are all involved with one another" (Kasimow, Sherwin, and Heschel, 1991, p. 6).

Summary

Our study of interreligious dialogue concluded in the spring of 2001 and thus predates the September 11 tragedy. However, we believe that the support for Nadira during her terrorism investigation after September 11 reflects the inspiration for understanding across religious borders from the participants and our own experiences. We strongly suggest that adult education research and practice embrace interreligious dialogue as a venue to expand the margins of adults' self-understanding from the perspective of religion. This will advance civil society by moving religious literacy in general and interreligious dialogue in particular from beyond the margins of our field and into the general river of discourse we now refer to as being about culture.

Expanding research into this area will help us to consider the extent to which our own religious experiences and assumptions, whether we embrace or reject them, serve as a lens through which we interpret our study of all aspects of adult learning and behavior. Engaging in interreligious dialogue as educators can help us learn about how religion informs the behaviors and assumptions of adult learners in professional, academic, and/or personal growth–oriented adult learning programs. Moving interreligious dialogue from the margins to the center will help us to be better program planners and teachers of adults.

References

Boys, M., and Lee, S. "The Catholic-Jewish Colloquium: An Experiment in Interreligious Learning." *Religious Education,* 1996, *91*(4), 420–466.

Charaniya, N. K., and Walsh, J. W. "Adult Learning in the Context of Interreligious Dialogue: A Collaborative Research Study with Christians, Jews, and Muslims." Unpublished doctoral dissertation, Department of Adult and Continuing Education, National-Louis University, 2001a.

Charaniya, N. K., and Walsh, J. W. "Adult Learning in the Context of the Interreligious Dialogue Process: Results of a Collaborative Research Study with Christians, Jews, and Muslims." Paper presented at the 42nd annual Adult Education Research Conference, East Lansing, Michigan, May 2001b.

Charaniya, N. K., and Walsh, J. W. "Interpreting the Experiences of Muslims, Christians, and Jews Engaged in Interreligious Dialogue: A Collaborative Research Study." *Religious Education,* 2001c, *96*(3), 351–368.

Daloz, L. "Transformation for the Common Good." In J. Mezirow and associates (eds.), *Learning as Transformation: Critical Perspectives on a Theory in Progress.* San Francisco: Jossey-Bass, 2000.

Dirkx, J. "Nurturing Soul in Adult Learning." In P. Cranton (ed.), *Transformative Learning in Action: Insights from Practice.* San Francisco: Jossey-Bass, 1997.

Eck, D. *Encountering God: From Bozeman to Banaras.* Boston: Beacon Press, 1993.

Elias, J. *The Foundations and Practice of Adult Religious Education.* Malabar, Fla.: Krieger, 1993.

English, L. M., and Gillen, M. A. (eds.). *Addressing the Spiritual Dimensions of Adult Learning: What Educators Can Do.* New Directions for Adult and Continuing Education, no. 85. San Francisco: Jossey-Bass, 2000.

Guy, T. (ed.). *Providing Culturally Relevant Adult Education: A Challenge for the Twenty-First Century.* New Directions for Adult and Continuing Education, no. 82. San Francisco: Jossey-Bass, 1999.

Hayes, E., and Colin, S. (eds.). *Confronting Racism and Sexism in Adult Education.* New Directions for Adult and Continuing Education, no. 61. San Francisco: Jossey-Bass, 1994.

Hayes, E., and Flannery, D. (eds.). *Women as Learners: The Significance of Learning in Adult Learning.* San Francisco: Jossey-Bass, 2000.

Hill, R. "Gay Discourse in Adult Education: A Critical Review." *Adult Education Quarterly,* 1995, *45*(3), 142–158.

Johnson-Bailey, J., and Cervero, R. "The Invisible Politics of Race in Adult Education." In E. Hayes and A. Wilson (eds.), *Handbook of Adult and Continuing Education.* San Francisco: Jossey-Bass, 2000.

Kasimow, H., Sherwin, B., and Heschel, J. *No Man Is an Island: Abraham Joshua Heschel and Interreligious Dialogue.* New York: Orbis Books, 1991.

Kegan, K. "What 'Form' Transforms: A Constructive-Developmental Approach to Transformational Learning." In J. Mezirow and associates (eds.), *Learning as Transformation: Critical Perspectives on a Theory in Progress.* San Francisco: Jossey-Bass, 2000.

Sheared, V., and Sissel, P. A. (eds.). *Making Space: Merging Theory and Practice in Adult Education.* New York: Bergin & Garvey, 2001.

Tisdell, E. J. *Creating Inclusive Adult Learning Environments: Insights from Multicultural Education and Feminist Pedagogy.* Collingdale, Pa.: Diane, 1995.

Tisdell, E. J. "Poststructural Feminist Pedagogies: The Possibilities and Limitations of a Feminist Emancipatory Adult Learning Theory and Practice." *Adult Education Quarterly,* 1998, *48*(3), 139–156.

Tisdell, E. J. "The Spiritual Dimensions of Adult Development." In C. M. Clark and R. S. Caffarella (eds.), *An Update on Adult Development Theory: New Ways of Thinking About the Life Course.* San Francisco: Jossey-Bass, 1999.

Tisdell, E. J. *Exploring Spirituality and Culture in Adult and Higher Education.* San Francisco: Jossey-Bass, 2003.

Walsh, J. W., and Charaniya, N. K. "Interpreting the Experiences of Muslims, Christians, and Jews Engaged in Interreligious Dialogue: A Collaborative Research Study." Paper presented at the annual conference of the Association of Professors and Researchers of Religious Education, Atlanta, Georgia, November 2000.

NADIRA K. CHARANIYA is assistant professor and coordinator of student services at the Los Angeles campus of Springfield College School of Human Services.

JANE WEST WALSH is a Jewish educator and consultant who specializes in facilitating values-based change processes with individuals, groups, and institutions.

4

To improve current civil society and achieve the possibilities globalization offers, we must incorporate an education-for-empowerment approach to lifelong learning. This chapter explores the potential, promise, and implications for local action and dialogue.

Supporting Change Through Local Action

Desi Larson

If adult educators are to have a positive effect on civil society, it is imperative we incorporate an education-for-empowerment approach to teaching and learning. This necessitates local action and dialogue. After addressing the role of adult education in promoting dialogue and action, I present an example of this in the field and conclude with discussion of the potential, promise, and implications of a critical approach to education, such as adult education espouses for building society. The discussion concludes with implications for practice.

The role of the adult educator is to facilitate learning and the reflection process, as opposed to merely providing information and resources. Brookfield (1987) proposes the following as principles of critical adult education: (1) voluntary participation, (2) respect for self-worth, (3) collaborative learning, (4) praxis (activity, reflection, and collaborative analysis), and (5) education to foster a spirit of critical reflection. Collaborative learning and reflective practice, assuming the social construction of knowledge and emphasizing process as part of debate, have roots in the work of progressive and emancipatory educators such as Addams ([1911] 1999), Dewey (1916), Freire (1992), Horton (Horton and Freire, 1990), and Lindeman (1926).

Without critical understanding of the workings of the state and the market, the interplay between them, and their effects on educational policy, some adult educators are left with an epistemology of adult education and

Acknowledgment: The author would like to recognize and thank the editors, as well as colleagues E. Michael Brady and Rosemary Mahoney, for their patient, thoughtful, and critical editorial feedback.

lifelong learning devoid of emancipatory content. A question that deserves serious consideration is this: To what degree is this lack of understanding due to the way adult educators are trained in adult education degree programs or to the real-world accommodation people need to make within the power structures within which they work? Further, what is the responsibility of adult education departments? Should adult educators be making accommodations or making change? Murphy (2000, p. 176) argues that we live not in a "learning society" but in a "post-learning society," where the policies of lifelong learning unwittingly pursue a post-learning society, in which emancipatory knowledge has lost its usefulness and ceased to play any productive or useful role in society.

What is our responsibility for this? And from where can we work? As an adult educator who embraces a critical and emancipatory paradigm, I believe that adult education programs must take advantage of their marginal position in both academe and in larger society and take the initiative to raise serious and challenging questions around policy and practice of adult education. Along with other adult educators in this tradition, I see adult education's marginal position as one of potential, requiring that we actively resist an increasingly homogenized, capitalistic world and continue to promote programs and people that value diversity, local action, and social change. Although many critical and important programs may be under attack in the current political and economic environment, it remains more critical than ever that, as a field, we do not succumb to co-optation. Building community and thinking outside the dominant culture becomes increasingly critical in a world reeling from the effects of environmental disasters and terrorism. Adult education sits at the margins of the world stage. The mainstream of just-in-time education and lifelong learning leave out the important pieces that build civil society and increase benefits to people, while enriching the corporations or corrupt governments. Margins become a place of potential, power, and change when we promote a critical understanding of the global economic context and emancipatory education.

The Role of Adult Education as Local Action

It would be irresponsible and naive to characterize adult learning as functioning entirely for the betterment of society. The need for skills development is real and necessary. However, to take an entirely utilitarian approach to adult education promises that we sell ourselves short and undermines our students' potential.

Regardless of what we might be teaching in adult education programs, precious few programs actually deliver the sort of learning experience that Phyllis Cunningham, John Dewey, bell hooks, Paulo Freire, Myles Horton, or other radical educators envisioned. However, opportunities exist at the margins; and some adult educators and programs have taken advantage of this. Radical ideas such as feminist pedagogy or emancipatory education are marginalized both in society at large and in the academy, which in turn relegates these programs to the margins of society. For example, human rights dialogue is generally bottom-up and is practically missing from the dominant discourse, although the drafters of the Universal Declaration of Human Rights (United Nations, 1948) envisioned people around the world learning about human rights; yet few people are even aware that this document exists.

We are at a critical juncture in history. Adult education can and must promote civil society. An emancipatory approach to lifelong learning facilitates authentic participation and addresses social issues. Emancipatory lifelong learning is best informed by the work of Paulo Freire. Freire's work was devoted to liberation of the most marginalized classes, with an approach to education that promoted action and social justice. Freire (1998) also highlighted the importance of education to human rights. He asked us to consider whether education was domesticating or liberating, and he (1985, p. 140) asserted that "education must be an instrument of transforming action, a political praxis at the service of permanent human liberation. This, let us repeat, does not happen only in the consciousness of people, but presupposes a radical change of structures, in which process consciousness will itself be transformed."

An educational approach that promotes a human rights culture meets resistance when others see it as running counter to educational agendas of governments and multinational corporations, which label human rights advocates as "subversive" or "leftist" (Brabeck and Rogers, 2000). Giroux (2001, p. 1) argues that a general complacency about and even hostility "toward addressing the basic problems of society" has led to a "rising indifference towards those aspects of education that foster critical consciousness." Clearly, this sort of resistance is a barrier to implementing emancipatory lifelong learning initiatives; and facilitators must acknowledge and overcome it.

Conservative and liberal educators alike recognize the need for lifelong learning in response to globalization and even recognize its potential to facilitate democratic dialogue, but it is the critical approach to lifelong learning that promotes local action and emancipatory knowledge (Murphy, 2000). As Horton and Freire (1990) pointed out, education can do one of two things: domesticate or liberate. A liberating approach will promote human rights agendas. "In the United States, humanist approaches to [lifelong learning] in the workplace can be devastating because they conceal the relationships of power to education leading to a reproductive practice of schooling where education and training become the servants of the corporations" (Cunningham, 2000, p. 578). Cunningham further argues that lifelong learning informed by a critical sociology "could be a concept on which to build education for all. As it now stands, it is divisive and drives education towards promoting commodity production not quality living" (p. 579). "What is needed now more than ever is a critical theory of lifelong learning that avoids half-baked theories of social change, and places educational policy within a world that is shaped by the force of modern capitalism" (Murphy, 2000, p. 177).

Initiative to Promote Local Action and Civil Society

Family literacy, or intergenerational literacy, is a fairly recent and innovative approach to adult education and community building. One agency that takes this approach is the Community Education Center and Home-based Instructional Program for Parents and Youth (CHIPPY) Even Start program, which serves at-risk families in a rural valley in northern New England. Even Start strives to provide a nurturing environment that emphasizes the growth and development of children and parents. The program is designed to build a sense of community among parents, children, and staff. This program is housed in a school in a remote region with 8 percent unemployment. The lack of employment opportunities and the low wages associated with available employment in the region likely contribute to the fact that over 25 percent of local residents over twenty-five years of age have not completed high school.

Between 1996 and 2001, more than 630 area residents were served in the district's Adult Basic Education program (now known as the Adult Education and Family Literacy Act—AEFLA) program. Nearly 60 percent of these participants were functioning at grade levels of 8.9 or lower in core subject areas and English as a second language (ESL) when they entered the program. Almost 20 percent were functioning at grade levels between 0.0 and 5.9 when they entered the program.

A study of this family literacy program indicates increased self-esteem and self-efficacy of participants (Larson and Caron, forthcoming). Interviews with school administrators produced a number of anecdotes of effects of participation that they had observed for CHIPPY learners. One school administrator noted that a parent who had been in an abusive relationship "finished her GED and is now in a nursing program. Her self-esteem is raised. Her children could've easily struggled [in school], but she's there for meetings and she's supportive at home" (Larson and Caron, forthcoming, p. 19). An elementary school principal interviewed related this observation: "Three years ago, when parents wanted to plan a day away from school to do something educational with their children, one of the CHIPPY staff would call me to make the arrangements. This year, my first call came from one of the CHIPPY parents [from the Parent Action Group]."

All administrators interviewed by Larson indicated that they were struck by the manner in which CHIPPY staff supported participants in school meetings, such as the Pupil Evaluation Team (PET) meetings. One administrator observed that "other program people talk for their clients. The CHIPPY staff are there [at the meeting] to support them, but they don't talk for them." The administrators all agreed that this approach helped learners to develop skills and dispositions necessary to advocate for themselves. Learners responded to open-ended responses in this section of the survey (Larson and Caron, forthcoming) with comments like these: "I never would have been able to speak in front of people [before CHIPPY]," and "I like how CHIPPY wants to hear your opinions and tries to work as a group."

Larson and Caron (forthcoming) identified adult education methods that CHIPPY staff used to promote critical thinking, learning, social engagement, and self-efficacy. Freire's liberatory pedagogy (1992) frames this, a pedagogy with three overlapping stages: (1) identification and use of program content that is meaningful for learners and reflects the local culture and issues; (2) codification and decodification of issues important to learners by learners; and (3) authentic, compassionate, and engaged reflective dialogue. The learner is always a cofacilitator and co-investigator in the process. Even Start represents the potential of a program that promotes dialogue and encourages local action.

Program Content Reflecting Local Culture and Issues

Freire (1992, p. 85) urges us to consider the local content and "concrete situation, reflecting the aspirations of the people." In their work with families, CHIPPY staff gear their efforts toward helping parents develop an understanding of child development, helping ease the successful transition of children to school, and helping support the positive interaction of parents with schools and the wider community, including the workplace. To foster critical reflection, adult learners participate actively in objectively assessing their family's needs and determining the level of services most suited to the need indicators that their families demonstrate.

Codification and Decodification

Another phase in Freire's liberatory education (1992), or pedagogy of the oppressed, revolves around codification and decodification. As Freire described in *Pedagogy of the Oppressed*, this stage can include concrete actions such as the learner writing evaluative essays that explore meanings and issues, essays in which a learner "relates how he perceived or felt a certain occurrence or situation" and can test assumptions about the situation or issues (p. 104). Although the CHIPPY program made no formal use of these sorts of methods, in retrospect many of the activities that CHIPPY educators and learners engaged in promoted similar kinds of critical reflection, evaluation, coding, and decoding.

Reflective Dialogue

Freire (1992, p. 56) describes liberatory practice as "co-intentional." Freire argues that authentic thinking and learning are possible for people but not things. Often the oppressed and self-depreciated feel and act more like objects than like people. Freire (p. 55) points out that "their situation has reduced them [the oppressed] to things. In order to regain their humanity they must cease to be things." To encourage continued asset identification and to help parents track and note the progress of their families and family members, including their own, both adult and child learners in the program maintain portfolios of authentic learning that they use, together with staff, to monitor and chart adult and child learners' progress toward their goals. In addition, to promote ongoing critical reflection, parents work with staff to regularly update comprehensive family action plans over the course of the program year.

Respecting Participants

CHIPPY staff members clearly respect participants. They search for strengths rather than deficits. According to one educator: "The program has so many doors for the learners and we as staff make sure that those doors get open. We're able to give them the support they need. One mother told me 'I started CHIPPY I felt like nobody, the staff accepted and respect me. Now, I feel like I am somebody and I'm going places.' Learners need to know they are capable of speaking for themselves and they are worthy—their opinions are worth something. It is so important to give them the opportunity to voice their opinions." (Larson and Caron, forthcoming, p. 24).

Freire (1992, pp. 79–80) describes true dialogue between learners and educators as built on deep respect and love: "Founding itself upon love, humility, and faith, dialogue becomes a horizontal relationship of which mutual trust between the dialoguers is the logical consequence." Freire (2000, p. 99) argues, "a dialogic relationship . . . is indispensable to knowledge." "Dialogue . . . is full of curiosity and unrest. It is full of mutual respect between the dialoging subjects."

Education as the Practice of Freedom

Education that is liberatory, what Freire (1992, p. 69) refers to as "education as the practice of freedom—as opposed to education as the practice of domination . . . considers . . . men in their relations with the world." People engaged in active learning and critical thinking have voice but also participate in relationship.

This process of praxis is perhaps nowhere more evident in the CHIPPY project design than in the parent action group—a hallmark of the program. A self-governing body open to all parents in the program, the parent action group is directed by a chair, vice chair, parliamentarian, secretary, and treasurer—all adult learners elected among their peers. Parent action group meetings are held weekly for the purpose of giving adult participants, among other responsibilities, the opportunity to give staff feedback on program operations and effectiveness; to select parent education topics; and to plan, coordinate, and carry out small and large group family gatherings, including family activity-based literacy experience outings.

Lessons Learned: Implications for Practice for Adult Education That Promotes Local Action

Some clear directives for critical practice emerge from a review of a program that promotes local action. Adult education should not be merely content- and skill-driven but also learner-driven and grassroots. Facilitators must evaluate and be critical of their own skills and share power with participants. It is also critical for facilitators to pay close attention to context, both locally and globally.

Content and Curricula. Freire (1992, p. 85) argues that what we teach and learn must be meaningful; it is essential that we make connections in our content "around present, existential, concrete situations, reflecting the aspirations of the people." When the focus is on basic skills or just-in-time learning, this element of meaningful learning is the first to disappear from the curriculum.

Facilitators' Skills. Facilitators must use a holistic mind-set and approach to their endeavors (Hart, 1997). We must promote authentic dialogue, reflection, and action, as well as cooperation between programs and with other programs and agencies. We also must be mindful not to ignore issues of power, social justice, and human rights, as happens in many lifelong learning initiatives, particularly those that are corporate- and government-driven. We must continuously reexamine our skills. This involves reflection, which is a crucial component of any critical adult education approach. Ewert and Grace (2000) remind us that facilitators need to practice facilitation, mobilization, and listening. This necessitates seeking to distribute and share power. Facilitators must avoid domestication, suppression, displacement, and devaluation of indigenous knowledge systems. As part of the process, facilitators should question ideologies present that produce and reproduce inequities (Stromquist, 2000).

Facilitators should also be cautious when evaluating and assessing their programs. Accountability is important, but the dignity of programs must not be compromised. In a capitalist context, the focus is on just-in-time approaches to education and training and to assessing outcomes. Program evaluation and educational assessment methods need to reflect the spirit of critical and transformative approaches to local action and community development—all of this requires time and resources. Adult education and community development facilitators must look for support and participate in global civil societies, which often are forms of resistance and offer the possibility of transformation (Hall, 1997). Examples of transnational civil society networks proliferate; they include environmental groups, peace organizations, and women's groups. Hall recommends that we get involved in already existing networks "working in the spirit of global society" (n.p.). However, we need to be intentional and reflective as we collaborate, being mindful of co-optation and understanding partners' motives around education and development.

Conclusion

In summary, if we truly want to promote civil society, we must promote local action. This is a tremendous challenge given the context of globalization, which has increased the gap between the wealthy and the poor, the strong and the weak. Adult education's position at the margins of the world stage is one that we must leverage. We must claim our place on the margins as a place of potential and change.

The engine of globalization works against civil society in many cases, but the program reviewed here gives evidence of the potential for a more human and humane world. When we promote a critical understanding of the global economic context and emancipatory education among practitioners in the field, programs develop that have profound implications for people and their communities. The example of the CHIPPY program demonstrates that successfully implementing local action is possible. Even more, it is increasingly imperative that lifelong learning promote civil society in the context of globalization. As Freire (1992, pp. 91–92) wrote, "Hope is rooted in men's incompletion, from which they move out in constant search—a search that can be carried out only in communion with others." We must continue striving to improve civil society and achieve the possibilities offered by globalization. To do this, an education-for-empowerment approach to lifelong learning that includes local action and dialogue is imperative.

References

Addams, J. *Twenty Years at Hull-House: With Autobiographical Notes*. New York: Signet, 1999. (Originally published 1911.)

Brabeck, M., and Rogers, L. "Human Rights as a Moral Issue: Lessons for Moral Educators from Human Rights Work." *Journal of Moral Education*, 2000, 29(2), 167–183.

Brookfield, S. *Developing Critical Thinkers: Challenging Adults to Explore Alternative Ways of Thinking and Acting*. San Francisco: Jossey-Bass, 1987.

Cunningham, P. "A Sociology of Adult Education." In E. Hayes and A. Wilson (eds.), *Handbook of Adult and Continuing Education*. San Francisco: Jossey-Bass, 2000.

Dewey, J. *Democracy and Education: An Introduction to the Philosophy of Education*. Old Tappan, N.J.: Macmillan, 1916.

Ewert, D. M., and Grace, K. "Adult Education for Community Action." In E. Hayes and A. Wilson (eds.), *Handbook of Adult and Continuing Education*. San Francisco: Jossey-Bass, 2000.

Freire, P. *The Politics of Education: Culture, Power, and Liberation*. New York: Bergin & Garvey, 1985.

Freire, P. *Pedagogy of the Oppressed*. New York: Continuum, 1992.

Freire, P. "Cultural Action for Freedom." *Harvard Educational Review*, 1998, *68*(4), 471–521.

Freire, P. *Pedagogy of the Heart*. New York: Continuum, 2000.

Giroux, H. "Pedagogy of the Depressed: Beyond the New Politics of Cynicism." *College Literature*, 2001, *28*(3), 1–32.

Hall, B. "Adult Learning, Global Civil Society, and Politics." Keynote speech for the Midwest Research-to-Practice Conference in Adult, Continuing and Community Education, East Lansing, Michigan, October 1997. [Available at http://www.anrecs.msu.edu/research/hallkey.htm.]

Hart, M. "Life-Affirming Work, Raising Children, and Education." *Convergence*, 1997, *30*(2/3), 128–136.

Horton, M., and Freire, F. *We Make the Road by Walking: Conversations on Education and Social Change*. Philadelphia: Temple University Press, 1990.

Larson, D., and Caron, P. "Freire and Family Literacy: Promoting Critical Thinking with an Engaged and Critical Approach to Learning." *INQUIRY: Critical Thinking Across the Disciplines*, forthcoming.

Lindeman, E. *The Meaning of Adult Education*. Montreal, Quebec: Harvest House, 1926.

Murphy, M. "Adult Education, Lifelong Learning, and the End of Political Economy." *Studies in the Education of Adults*, 2000, *32*(2), 166–181.

Stromquist, N. "Voice, Harmony, and Fugue in Global Feminism." *Gender and Education*, 2000, *12*(4), 419–433.

United Nations. "Universal Declaration of Human Rights." [http://www.un.org/Overview/rights.html], 1948.

DESI LARSON is an associate professor of Adult Education and Women's Studies at the University of Southern Maine.

5

This chapter addresses the contradictions inherent to working at the confluence of human resource development and adult education, as well as the opportunity for transformation in the workplace.

Envisioning Change from the Margins Within: Human Resource Development (HRD) and Corporate Downsizing

Daniela Truty

Adult education and human resource development (HRD) are marginalized fields within the academic and corporate contexts (Belzer and others, 2001). Additionally, HRD professionals may become marginalized from the authentic self as they carry out harmful executive demands (Stanage, 1974, 1981; Truty, 2003b). The literature on institutionalization and deinstitutionalization (DiMaggio and Powell, 1983; Dacin, Goodstein, and Scott, 2002; Greenwood, Suddaby, and Hinings, 2002; Kraatz and Moore, 2002; Thornton, 2002) suggests that power can be located at the confluence of adult education and HRD when practice is reframed into a force for positive organizational change.

I have learned from my experience in corporate HRD that committed professionals can expand the traditional margins to improve the lives of people working in corporations. To illustrate, I will tell a story of how twenty-eight white-collar workers experienced what some call involuntary separation as a result of a corporate downsizing action at TREBCO (a pseudonym), a large U.S. manufacturing firm. This story draws from a 2001 qualitative study in which I was a researcher-participant; I had been employed at TREBCO as an adult educator–HRD professional and ultimately was downsized as well (Truty, 2003b). This story is also shaped by my dual perspectives, acquired through adult education graduate study and my work experience in HRD; it uses a journal of my observations and sensemaking process as the primary data source. I conclude this chapter with

NEW DIRECTIONS FOR ADULT AND CONTINUING EDUCATION, no. 104, Winter 2004 © Wiley Periodicals, Inc.

implications and suggestions for converting HRD into a potential place for emancipatory adult education.

The Story: Set in TREBCO's HRD Department

One day rumors began to circulate that institutional shareholders had expressed their dismay to TREBCO's CEO about unsatisfactory corporate performance for third-quarter earnings. Within days the CEO launched a strategic review of all organizational processes. Despite focus groups and departmental meetings to identify options for process improvement, TREBCO's executive leaders announced that some employee action would soon take place. Senior employees who had survived the past seven downsizing actions at the company explained that *employee action* meant downsizing again—that is, some workers would lose their jobs.

Mirroring this announcement from executive leaders, the HRD department manager informed the team that regrettably two members would be "affected," a situation that was "very, very sad," he admitted, because "this group [had] become *family* and [had] come together nicely as a team" (journal entry, Aug. 25, 2000). Instantly, the team yielded to silent suspicion and incessant speculation. Who will it be? This question, spoken or not, echoed beyond the HRD department and throughout the organization (Truty, 2003b). Uncertain of their future and fearful of the unknown, many found their workflow disrupted.

During the days leading to the downsizing action, trapped in this eerie environment, I suddenly had ample time to observe, think, and reflect. Current employee projects lost purpose and meaning because we did not know whether or not the company would complete, shelve, or even drop our projects.

One day I noticed that the HRD manager seemed to have new responsibilities. He was customizing an instructional design piece in collaboration with the outplacement consulting firm TREBCO had hired. I excitedly complied with his request for pointers on how to deal effectively with learner resistance in the training intervention that he was designing. I later discovered that it was intended to teach supervisors how to downsize staff the legal way.

Nevertheless, this was a positive sign for me, I reasoned. The manager had invited me, and not some other departmental colleague, to provide input for a module that he was designing. I must be part of the in-group! In this predownsizing climate, when organizational communication was missing, partial, or shrouded, many of us sought signs that might foretell what our own fate might be. I assisted the department administrator in finding an external contact who would quickly and competently produce job aids that supervisors would use while permanently separating employees from the job (the company's term for "laying off"). I even hand-delivered a pack of these documents to an HRD manager who needed them to conduct downsizing training for supervisors working in a neighboring state. Pursuit of belonging with, and acceptance by, those more powerful than I seemed not only politically wise but also required for survival. Citizenship among the in-group offered much-needed solace and reassurance amid the stifling surrealism of this difficult time.

Fleeting twinges of conscience resurfaced insistently and compelled me to ask myself: Who are you? At what point will you say no? Numb and emotionless, I was forced to admit that for the corporate person whom I had become the answer was probably never. I sensed that I was complicit in this premeditated process, but internal questions prevented a more honorable reply. Flashing quickly in and out of consciousness, some questions appeared too uncomfortable to answer in ways that threatened the status quo. What would I say to my significant other, who had grown to appreciate the lifestyle that this job could afford? This was a relatively new career for me as a reentry woman. Where would I find another job such as this? I did not want to be searching right now. When D-day arrived, I was shocked to learn that I too was "regrettably affected" (Truty, 2003b, p. 109).

Reflective Aftermath: Making Meaning of the Event

Jobless, I had time to return to scholarly roots in adult education. I designed a qualitative study, which later became my dissertation, to understand my experience of this downsizing event as well as those of my separated colleagues. Twenty-eight employees whom TREBCO downsized participated in this study via interviews and observation. I participated through the journal that I had been keeping.

Findings

Participants described four broad experiences of the same downsizing event: "the layoff was a godsend"; "opportunity came"; "it happened, move on"; and "we were hurt" (Truty, 2003b, p. 150). Everyone was sent away instead of freely choosing to leave; however, along the continuum of readiness to leave, those in "the layoff was a godsend" category welcomed the event. At the other end, those in the "we were hurt" category were devastated. Those in the "godsend" and "opportunity" categories had no plans to stay for the long term, although the sense of urgency to leave varied among them. Those in the "godsend" category indicated that they would have left out of necessity, because the most recent job situation had been destructive to their health and well-being. They had struggled to resolve difficulties and to hang on, but ultimately they were defeated. Those in the "opportunity" category would have left when they were ready because this job was a stepping-stone in their overall careers. Members of this group shared a sense of financial independence and confidence in their employability. However, the timing of their move was not their own.

Coming to an Understanding

In interpreting the data, I understood that downsizing could not have occurred without the support of a complex network of cultural institutions that have shaped the public's perception that a downsizing action is tolerable or even acceptable (Galtung, 1990; Truty, 2002). For example, the Employment at Will Doctrine, which many states enforce, allows employers and employees to terminate a work relationship unilaterally for whatever reason they choose (Truty, 2003b). The media, with its casual and repetitive reporting of downsizing actions, desensitizes the public to the impact on people's lives and contributes to the perception that there is no alternative (Swift, 1999). Dominant ideologies or -*isms*, such as capitalism, consumerism, competitivism, and individualism, as well as language and scientific measurement, have a huge role in this complicity. Diluted words, such as *downsizing, business process re-engineering, process improvement, strategic review,* and *rightsizing,* diminish the impact of taking the job away; and scientific measurement, evaluation, and prediction of economic trends in the industry reinforce that expert knowledge trumps people's fears and experience (Galtung, 1990; Truty, 2002, 2003b). In sum, a multitude of factors legitimize unilateral corporate decisions to take the employee's livelihood away (Truty, 2002, 2003b).

I also realized that despite the optimism with which some depict the protean career, such as stressing career over job, frequent job change, and reduced commitment to a specific employer (Truty, 2003a), some study participants experienced betrayal and frustration when TREBCO failed to meet their long-held expectations of employment security and reciprocity. Many were not surprised that TREBCO had acted as it did. With additional probing, some listed ways in which TREBCO might have downsized costs and even staff without sending people away (Truty, 2002, 2003b).

I sadly reflected on my colleagues' stories of hurt, exclusion, rejection, betrayal, fear, apprehension, and loss. The training I had done to promote employee involvement, high-performance culture, self-directed work teams, empowerment, accountability, performance management, values, guiding behaviors, and respect for people now appeared manipulative and laden with secret agendas. In fact, these forms of training urged employees to identify with coworkers at TREBCO, only to send them away during the downsizing event.

Repulsion

My journal revealed repulsion from the HRD profession in general—and specifically from the strategic review team who planned and then implemented the downsizing. Day in, day out, during the weeks leading up to the separations, I watched representatives from other departments—corporate and outlying human resources, corporate communications, and corporate counsel—convening inside a secluded room not far from my cubicle. I knew about the general discussions that were taking place, but information stopped short of stating particulars.

In one journal entry I wrote, "given what I have experienced, and given the pain that I have seen, how can I possibly return to this HRD world?" I was distraught because I believed that not only had I been separated from the job at TREBCO but also from my recently chosen career. I no longer wanted to be affiliated with the HRD profession that had clearly been instrumental in teaching supervisors how to hurt employees. I wondered how I could be true to myself and capitalize on the experience gained through my most recent career (Truty, 2003b).

Attraction

With the passage of time and further reflection, a reframed perspective on HRD practice emerged. Instead of viewing HRD as an implementer, I began to envision ways in which two major influences from marginalized positions might come together in a powerful synthesis to effect positive change within the workplace. Newscasts and documentaries suggested that Southwest Airlines, for example, retained profitability during this economic recession; it had not downsized by firing the staff. A possibility existed, therefore, that kinder and gentler alternatives were available to navigate times of economic uncertainty. Additionally, as a member of a privileged demographic group, that is, white, middle-class, and partly supported by a significant other, I was not dependent on my HRD position for financial well-being; thus, I could assume risks that others could not. In this marginalized midrank corporate position, I could be true to myself while chipping away at oppressive workplace conditions because I had little to lose. By honing my skills at persuasion and effective communication, I could access the organization's core decision-making group instead of intentionally steering away. I could reframe my position from HRD-professional-as-implementer to HRD-professional-as-actor by learning to communicate upward and challenging my resistance toward joining the organizational core group.

Power and Change from the Margins Within

Combining perspectives from adult education and HRD, I could derive my power from the margins of the corporation and the confluence with the wider business society in which it exists. To my HRD role, I could bring knowledge about social movements, worker development, and emancipatory learning to guide discussions with those at the organizational core. Such discussions are made possible by using the language of performativity, which corporate managers use to convey their concerns about efficiency, performance, input, output, and all that contributes to improving the organizational bottom line (Burbules and Callister, 2000). As a critical outsider,

I could easily be dismissed as a voice too dissonant even to gain the core group's attention. However, by working from within, assisting the organization to achieve reasonable goals, I earn the potential to make my dissenting views heard.

Embracing my position at the margins where fast-paced competitors and institutional pressures are rarely found may be a way to deinstitutionalize corporate dominance and shareholder supremacy. A midorganizational level HRD position is not important enough for many to covet (except perhaps those at lower organizational rungs). The literature on deinstitutionalization suggests that it is in the margins, where less is at stake, that exploration and innovative solutions can sometimes take shape (Dacin, Goodstein, and Scott, 2002; Greenwood, Suddaby, and Hinings, 2002; Kleiner, 2002; Kraatz and Moore, 2002; Thornton, 2002). At the confluence of two marginalized professions lie the power and freedom to quietly and systematically effect positive change.

Thus, an adult education and HRD professional can have options for influencing change from the margins within by doing the following:

- Elevating marginalized corporate stakeholders, including employees, to more prominent influential status. This could be accomplished through research, writing, and dissemination of findings about their experiences across professional boundaries, thereby penetrating competing perspectives and casting doubt on unproblematized truths (Dacin, Goodstein, and Scott, 2002; Greenwood, Suddaby, and Hinings, 2002; Kleiner, 2002; Truty, 2002, 2003b).
- Using the potential of varied contexts where adult learning occurs—including the organizational front porch to which smokers are relegated, corporate hallways, and even the restrooms—and transforming them into sites for researching, generating, and promoting discourses of power, resistance, and possibility (Truty, 2003b).
- Modeling simplicity to resist powerful urges for incessant consumption.
- Contributing realistic, credible, and valuable theory and scholarship about the workplace for policy creation, advocacy, and implementation (Truty, 2002, 2003b).
- Developing a repertoire of shared tools, skills, and techniques from adult education and HRD to use toward positive change in the workplace.

Summary

In summary, human resource developers may participate in the study of adult education and become shaped by its ideals. Within the corporation HRD is frequently practiced at midorganizational levels, where professionals hold just enough power and visibility to implement decision-maker mandates. At the same time, the human resource developer stops short of feeling powerful enough to question the status quo and be true to him- or herself. Tempted by comfortable salary and perquisites, the HRD professional might elect to comply with decision makers' demands only to find him- or herself in the throes of a troubled relationship with personal identity—particularly if one is also a scholar of adult education. Therefore, an additional layer of marginalization occurs when the self is separate from the way that one chooses to act. When difficult situations demanding HRD assistance arise, such as corporate downsizing via involuntary separations, the HRD professional may subsequently be tempted to veer clear of the HRD and corporate professions due to personal conflict with what should be versus what is. However, power to effect positive change in the workplace may be found at the confluence of two marginal perspectives embodied by the HRD professional with roots in adult education. In that unique position, the HRD professional informed by adult education can perfect communicative skills already developed to navigate the midlevel position to access core decision-making organizational groups. In this newfound position, having gained decision makers' attention, one is poised to introduce ideals of adult education. Skilled as a researcher and passionate about people at the edges of workplace and external society, the HRD practitioner can give voice to the worker and project it across disciplinary boundaries. Quietly but systematically, the HRD professional can effect positive change from the margins within toward enhanced worker well-being.

Afterword

The observant reader will probably note that I presently teach HRD in academia instead of practicing it in the corporation. With a doctorate in adult continuing education and an emphasis in HRD, I had an opportunity to shape the minds of those who would practice the profession in a corporate context. Working within the less prestigious college of education instead of the college of business, I embrace the freedom to share my learning and tale about the emancipatory potential of an informed and critical HRD professional working from the margins of the corporation. More than ever, I am aware of the importance of my dual perspectives in my students' formation. Corporate executives and respected organizational consultants introduce innovative trends and institutionalized truths learned through intercompany migration and membership in professional associations (Kraatz and Moore, 2002). Likewise, I believe that these HRD students carry with them lessons learned from my grounded experiential and theoretical knowledge to influence corporate change from organizational margins.

References

Belzer, A., and others. "HRD on the Margins: Exploring Resistance to HRD in Adult Education." Paper presented at the Adult Education Research Conference, East Lansing, Michigan, June 2001.

Burbules, N. C., and Callister Jr., T. A. "Universities in Transition: The Promise and the Challenge of New Technologies." *Teachers College Record,* 2000, *102*(2), 271–293.

Dacin, M. T., Goodstein, J., and Scott, W. R. "Institutional Theory and Institutional Change: Introduction to the Special Research Forum." *Academy of Management Journal,* 2002, *45*(1), 45–56.

DiMaggio, P. J., and Powell, W. W. "The Iron Cage Revisited: Institutional Isomorphism and Collective Rationality in Organizational Fields." *American Sociological Review,* 1983, *48*(2), 147–160.

Galtung, J. "Cultural Violence." *Journal of Peace Research,* 1990, 27(3), 291–305.

Greenwood, R., Suddaby, R., and Hinings, C. R. "Theorizing Change: The Role of Professional Associations in the Transformation of Institutionalized Fields." *Academy of Management Journal,* 2002, *45*(1), 58–79.

Kleiner, A. "Core Group Therapy." *Strategy + Business,* 2002, Q2, 1–4.

Kraatz, M. S., and Moore, J. H. "Executive Migration and Institutional Change." *Academy of Management Journal,* 2002, *45*(1), 120–143.

Stanage, S. M. (ed.). *Reason and Violence: Philosophical Investigation.* Totowa, N.J.: Littlefield, Adams & Co., 1974.

Stanage, S. M. "Order, Violatives, and Metaphors of Violence." *Thought: A Review of Culture and Idea,* 1981, *56*(200), 89–100.

Swift, R. "Propaganda." *New Internationalist Magazine,* 1999, *314.* [http://www.newint.org/issue314/world.htm].

Thornton, P. H. "The Rise of the Corporation in a Craft Industry: Conflict and Conformity in Institutional Logics." *Academy of Management Journal,* 2002, *45*(1), 81–101.

Truty, D. "Corporate Downsizing: Institutionalized Myth and Implications for Resistance." Paper presented at the 21st annual Midwest Research-to-Practice Conference in Adult, Continuing and Community Education, DeKalb, Illinois, Oct. 2002.

Truty, D. "Challenging the Lure of the Protean Career." Paper presented at the 22nd annual Midwest Research-to-Practice Conference in Adult, Continuing and Community Education, Columbus, Ohio, Oct. 2003a.

Truty, D. "Do I Count? Adult Experiences with Involuntary Separation from the Job: Context, Perspective, Violence, and Institutionalized Myth." Unpublished doctoral dissertation, Department of Counseling, Adult, and Higher Education, Northern Illinois University, 2003b.

DANIELA TRUTY is an assistant professor of Human Resource Development at Northeastern Illinois University.

6

This chapter addresses the dual status of African American faculty in adult education as both a marginalized group and as a group central to the collective identity of adult education in the United States.

Insider and Outsider Status: An African American Perspective

Sherwood Smith

Although many social factors contribute to marginalization, race may be the most cogent given its place in the interconnected web of oppression (Frye, 2003; Lorde, 2000). African Americans experience racism no matter their other group identities. For instance, my identity as an adult educator is predicated on my being African American, male, from a working-class family, a first-generation college graduate, and heterosexual. However, my skin color visually defines my marginalized status in the academy in the United States.

African American faculty members are a marginalized force in adult education (Colin and Preciphs, 1991; Peterson, 1996; Neufeldt and McGee, 1990). However, as this chapter shows, they are central to the field's collective identity in the United States. This chapter first addresses factors that contribute to African Americans' marginalization and then addresses those factors that contribute to the power gained at the margins.

African American Faculty in Higher Education

African Americans are underrepresented as tenured or tenure-track faculty in general and in adult education. Although 12 percent of the U.S. population, African Americans represent only 5 percent of all faculty members in higher education, and they disproportionately occupy lower ranks than their Caucasian counterparts (Harvey, 2002). Moreover, African Americans were awarded only 6 percent of all 27,888 doctoral degrees in 2000 (Harvey, 2002). African Americans have made greater strides in educational fields, as the percentage of earned doctorates equaled their 12 percent representation U.S. population that year.

57

This underrepresentation may reflect issues of power and privilege within the larger society (Banks, 1995; Collins, 2000; Hugo, 1990; Turner and Meyers, 1999). Giroux (1985, p. 35) explains power as "a form of cultural production, linking agency and structure through the ways in which public and private representations are concretely organized and structured." Such underrepresentation has several consequences for how African American faculty can function in the academy. For instance, it reinforces the false stereotype that African Americans cannot or do not succeed in higher education while minimizing the multiple barriers they face and overcome. Underrepresentation also limits the number of peer mentors and further reduces recruitment and retention of new African American faculty (Blackwell, 1989, 1996; Holland, 1993; Witt, 1990). For example, Blackwell's study (1983, p. 19) of 157 African American education professionals found "one way to communicate to outsider groups (i.e., Whites) that they have a shot at success is to provide visible role models of success for them." Finally, while working with African American faculty can challenge mainstream stereotypes and prejudices (Jackson, 1991; Nelson, 2002) as outsiders, African Americans still must draw strength from family and friends outside the university community to succeed in their faculty role.

African American Issues in Adult Education Research

To identify African American faculty's influence on scholarship in adult education, I examined four sources—the annual Adult Education Research Conference (AERC) online listings, the journal *Adult Education Quarterly,* and two computerized databases (ERIC and *Dissertation Abstracts*)—to assess the degree of scholarship focusing on African Americans and adult education.

A review of AERC online listings from 1992 through 2000 found 37 of 638 presentations focusing on issues related to African Americans. Notably, the most presentations on African American topics were in 1993 and 1994 (seven of sixty presentations in 1993 and seven of seventy-three in 1994). This bump may have resulted from the first two African American preconferences (held before the AERC meetings) in those years. Later such preconferences may not have boosted the number of African American–related papers at AERC, as by then the first cohort of African American scholars had other forums for their work. Further exploration into the communication within that first cohort is needed to better explain the 1993 and 1994 bump in African American–related AERC papers. Second, a review of the *Adult Education Quarterly* from 1992 to 1998 and from 2001 through 2003 yielded only nineteen article titles related to African Americans, of 290 articles published. Notably, twelve (60 percent) of the nineteen were published from 2001 to 2003, which coincided with a change of editors whose perspectives may have influenced article selection.

Third, an ERIC database search of journal articles in English between 1993 and 2004 using a Boolean keyword search strategy of "adult education" yielded 6,335 articles, but a search combining "African American or black" with "adult education" found only seventy-five (or 1.2 percent) of all 6,335 adult education articles). Finally, a search of *Dissertation Abstracts Online* limited to English between 1993 and 2003 using "adult education" in the title and the keyword "African-American" or "black" yielded 126 items, or 20 percent of all 625 adult education dissertations. This is a promising trend for growing scholarship in this area. Although the previously mentioned search strategies may not have caught all items related to African Americans and adult education, they suggest that research and publications directly related to African Americans has been increasing.

African American Faculty Experience Adult Education Departments

The limited number of ten African American tenure-track faculty members in adult education calls into question the supposed inclusiveness of our field (Ross-Gordon, 1991; Way, 1992). (Without a formal count of African American faculty in adult education, I used professional contacts to get an approximate number.) The lack of diversity among faculty members conflicts with the roles of leadership and change agent that adult educators lay claim to in the face of the reality of a multicultural society in the United States. Over time authors (Byndon, 1992; Courtney, 1989; Jensen, Liveright, and Hallenbeck, 1964; Ross-Gordon, 1991) have addressed the importance of welcoming all people in adult education. Colin and Preciphs (1991) describe academic racism as both a social and a structural problem and acknowledge that it is critical for adult educators to examine how racism affects education.

In 1991 Ross-Gordon exposed the lack of a multicultural presence in adult education's written texts. A variety of works discuss the historical absence of African American voices in education literature and research: *Education of the African American Adult: A Historical Overview* (Neufeldt and McGee, 1990) and *Making Space* (Sheared and Sissel, 2001). Conflicts and contradictions in adult education are not new. Lindeman's work *The Meaning of Adult Education* (1926), written by a white male professor, did not reflect diverse voices yet called for inclusiveness. Adult education, despite its claim of progressive roots, still has a tradition of systematically marginalizing people of color. The system of adult education within higher education functions to maintain the status quo (Manning, 2000) while claiming to support social change and acknowledge privilege.

Challenges for Adult Education Faculty

My own research found that a complex structure of challenges and rewards impacts African American faculty in adult education. African American faculty overall described their key challenges as the following: being expected to serve on committees and to be involved with students more than their white peers; lacking senior faculty who could share their research interests or be role models and advocates within the field and institution; and being challenged daily about their knowledge, during which "people tried to dismiss or diminish them" (Smith, 1995, p. 122). They reported that the rewards for working in the academy included success in meeting challenges to their knowledge and position; positive feelings of seeing their students succeed; and being true to the African American community, their family, their personal values, and religion (Taylor-Archer and Smith, 2002).

Perhaps most importantly, African American faculty members want their institutions to acknowledge their challenges and contributions within the tenure processes. Thus, marginality provided African American faculty with both rewards and frustrations related to peers, students, and staff. When they dealt successfully with frustrating or racist situations, African American faculty experienced efficacy and affirmation (Bell, 1992; Taylor-Archer and Smith, 2002).

Challenging Constructions of Prejudice and Marginality

"Barriers have different meanings to those on opposite sides of them, even though they are barriers to both" (Frye, 2003, p. 205). Barriers in the academy are most noticeable in the lack of representation in positions and scholarship. The early antiracist work of African American adult educators is described in *Freedom Road* by Peterson (1996), a collection of essays that had disappeared from mainstream literature (Peters and Jarvis, 1991; Jensen, Liveright, and Hallenbeck, 1964) and only recently reappeared as a result of direct action of writers from the margins such as Colin, Guy, Peterson, Sheared, and others.

In 1991 African Americans and their allies in the adult education community convened a "series of African-American adult education research symposia" (Peterson, 1996, p. xii). These included separate events to create space for African American voices, issues, and concerns to be heard; and they culminated with the first African American preconferences at the AERC in 1993 and 1994. Organizing a preconference demonstrates that African Americans recognized the absence of our stories. From the margins they created a place to promote an antiracist and social justice agenda within the formal AERC structure. Using the preconference put the agenda within AERC's formal institutional support structure to attract colleagues involved in the main conference, while creating a space for younger African American faculty and graduate students to network.

Construction of Prejudice and Privilege

As an African American faculty member, I have been mistaken for the waiter at a university professional development workshop and listened to my white colleagues complain that other African Americans were given administrative positions solely based on race. Similar daily experiences of African American faculty (Gregory, 1999; Bonner, 2004) illustrate that marginality is embedded in individual and institutional attitudes and behaviors (Hayes and Colin, 1994). Indeed, "Within the field of adult education the ability to serve all members of society continues to be a vision not yet realized" (Ross-Gordon, 1990, p. 5). The meaning of power and discrimination at the system level are best described as an "invisible knapsack of privileges" (McIntosh, 2000, p. 184). Members of the dominant group are often unconscious and unaware of their privileges, especially at the cultural and institutional level (Sue and Sue, 1990; Tatum, 2003; Yamato, 2000) and thus are unable to recognize their culture, power, privilege, and prejudice. Prejudice can be as simple as an individual making a verbal slur or as complex as institutional beliefs about qualifications based only on physical appearance. Thus, racial and ethnic bias (Nelson, 2002) results in an unwelcoming and unsupportive work environment for faculty of color (Turner and Meyers, 1999) that forces African American faculty to the margins.

Power at the Margins

However, power is gained at the margins. To navigate the academy, African American faculty members must become fluent in the cultural contexts of the mainstream and the margins. Through this added burden, they develop multiple levels of consciousness and several frames of reference from which to critique adult education. As Gregory (1999, p. 112) notes, "There is a presumption that because we've reached the level of an academic . . . that we've become acculturated. There's a lot of energy that goes into contemplating your own differences compared to other peoples' experiences."

Changing the Gatekeepers: The Outsider Within. The level of satisfaction and ability to transform the margins depends on one's personal experience as a scholar and relationships with other African American colleagues. For instance, African American faculty must act at both the margins and the center to meet the three criteria for tenure and promotion: research, teaching, and service. They are frequently called upon to act as the ethnic expert or spokesperson and to speak as if there is a singular identity. Meanwhile, they challenge stereotypes and dominant constructions of race through their teaching, research, and service activities. However, when African American faculty members focus on ethnic identity and race issues, they risk being labeled as ethnic rather than pure scholars (Carr and Kemmis, 1986; Gregory, 1999; Ross-Gordon, 1991; Tisdell, 1993). Ultimately, expanding the margins will require moving beyond the storytelling and theory building of the academy. The next step is to make social change in the world that requires the construction of new knowledge (Cunningham, 1989; Ross-Gordon, 1990; Sheared and Sissel, 2001).

Changing the Center from the Margins. The African American pre-conferences at the AERC created a forum in 1993 to expand research, publications, and scholarship and to facilitate peer communication, mentoring relationships, and role modeling. The preconference outpost at the margins of an established professional event eventually influenced the center by supporting publications (for example, *Making Space* by Sheared and Sissel, 2001); by understanding African American faculty issues and scholarship; and by sharing information about job opportunities, publications, and professional development events.

African American faculty members confront largely positivist, dominant discourse in the academy through their scholarship on non-Eurocentric perspectives, service to marginalized communities, and presence in the classroom. Doing so creates "psychic disequilibrium," as Adrienne Rich describes in *The Feminist Classroom* (1994, p. 1): "When those who have the power to name and to socially construct reality choose not to see you, hear you, whether you are dark-skinned, old, disabled, female, or speak with a different accent or dialect than theirs, when someone with the authority of a teacher, say, describes the world and you are not in it, there is a moment of psychic disequilibrium, as if you looked into a mirror and saw nothing."

However, embracing the power, with its psychic disequilibrium, from confronting the dominant discourse can lead to tokenism.

Tokenism in the Academy

Service for African American faculty means acting as a cultural informant, facilitator, or mediator. This role simultaneously tokenizes and empowers African American faculty. I serve on committees to add a diverse perspective; therefore, I gain access to decision-making processes at higher levels than many of my white colleagues. At the same time, I am silenced because of my status as marginal, invisible, or the token minority. African American faculty members are agents of cultural change within academic adult education both because and in spite of our marginalized status. Marginal status can serve as cultural capital at the intersection of social justice and adult education. African American faculty brings silenced perspectives and voices to the table. Although providing access to the dominant framework, this role can be costly because we risk being viewed as tools of the establishment.

However, with caveats, we can leverage this ambiguous position to gain perspective on adult education's dominant paradigms and to promote transformative learning for our colleagues and students. Colleagues and administrators seek our views as faculty insiders and as people of color outsiders (Cose, 1993; Gregory, 1999). Our mere physical presence in the classroom, as African American scholars, challenges deep-seated assumptions and thus impacts learning well beyond the syllabus. To avoid becoming a tool of oppression, however, we must not lose sight of the academy's hegemonic nature (Cunningham, 1989; Manning, 2000), which is all too willing to promote token African Americans, such as Sowell (1981), Steele (1990), and

Spring (2001). In sum, true African American faculty power derives from representing a diversity of experiences and beliefs, which create a transformative learning experience (Mezirow, 1978) that deconstruct racist stereotypes (Banks, 1995; Cose, 1993; Manglitz, 2003.

Conclusion

University adult education programs are generally small, yet they foster marginalized communities. African American faculty members have alleviated isolation and created power at the margins through meetings, conferences, and other off-campus events that bring together African American faculty. They act intentionally at the margins to expand and reshape the borders and deconstruct gates. People and fields at the margins are more likely to respond to members who act as change agents. In adult education this is through the scholarly activities of research, teaching, and service, as well as through personal acts that further social justice. African American faculty members' experiences of isolation and marginalization, as seen from the outsider's vantage point, create a special lens that exposes the potential for adult education to empower all people. As a field of practice, adult education's stated valuing of learners and their lived experience increases the possibility that the actions of African American faculty might influence the field (Cunningham, 1989; Hiemstra, 1991; Mezirow, 1978).

The ideas of andragogy and transformation can bring innovation and opportunity to the field (Peterson, 1996). Leadership from marginalized groups impacts the overall character of adult education through books and articles, which can introduce missing voices when used in classes. Marginalized voices have and will continue to impact the field through presentations and seminars at professional conferences to change the understanding of what has gotten adult education to where it is today and where it will be in the future. The challenge that we as African American faculty experience in finding our place and voice is within the view of "the liberal integrationist [who] always assumed that blacks had to succeed in the context of white institutions and Euro-American standards . . . and that 'academic standard' should not be held hostage to political agendas" (Manning, 2000, p. 14).

References

Banks, J. "The Historical Reconstruction of Knowledge About Race." *Educational Researcher,* 1995, 24(3), 15–22.

Bell, D. *Faces at the Bottom of the Well: The Permanence of Racism.* New York: Basic Books, 1992.

Blackwell, J. "Mentoring: An Action Strategy for Increasing Minority Faculty." *Academe,* 1989, 75, 8–14.

Blackwell, J. *Networking and Mentoring: A Study of Cross-Generational Experience of Blacks in Graduate and Professional Schools.* 13 July, 1996. (ED 235 745). [Available from http://md1.csa.com/csa/factsheets/eric.shtml.]

Blackwell, J. E. *Networking and Mentoring: A Study of Cross-Generational Experiences of Blacks in Graduate and Professional Schools.* Report No. HE016725. Atlanta: Southern Educational Foundation, 1983.

Bonner II, F. A. "Black Professor: On the Track but out of the Loop." *Chronicle of Higher Education: Chronicle Review,* 2004, *50*(40), B11.

Byndon, A. "Questions and Issues Related to a Lack of Multicultural Research in Adult Education." Paper presented at the Midwest Research-to-Practice Conference, Manhattan, Kansas, Oct. 1992.

Carr, W., and Kemmis, S. *Becoming Critical.* Philadelphia: Falm Press, 1986.

Cervero, R. M., and Wilson, A. L. *Planning Responsibly for Adult Education: A Guide to Negotiating Power and Interests.* San Francisco: Jossey-Bass, 1994.

Colin III, S., and Preciphs, T. "Perceptual Patterns and the Learning Environment: Confronting White Racism." In R. Hiemstra (ed.), *Creating Environments for Effective Adult Learning.* New Directions for Adult and Continuing Education, no. 50. San Francisco: Jossey-Bass, 1991.

Collins, P. *Black Feminist Thought: Knowledge, Consciousness, and the Politics of Empowerment.* New York: Routledge, 2000.

Cose, E. *The Rage of a Privileged Class.* New York: HarperCollins, 1993.

Courtney, S. "Defining Adult and Continuing Education." In S. Merriam and P. Cunningham (eds.), *Handbook of Adult and Continuing Education.* San Francisco: Jossey-Bass, 1989.

Cunningham, P. "Making a More Significant Impact on Society." In B. A. Quigley (ed.), *Fulfilling the Promise of Adult and Continuing Education.* New Directions for Continuing Education, no. 44. San Francisco: Jossey-Bass, 1989.

Frye, M. "Oppression." In K. E. Rosenblum and T. M. Travis (eds.), *The Meaning of Difference: American Constructions of Race, Sex and Gender, Social Class, and Sexual Orientation.* (3rd ed.) New York: McGraw-Hill, 2003.

Giroux, H. "Critical Pedagogy, Cultural Politics, and the Discourse of Experience." *Journal of Education,* 1985, *167,* 22–41.

Gregory, S. T. *Black Women in the Academy: The Secrets to Success and Achievement.* Lanham, Md.: University Press of America, 1999.

Harvey, W. *Minorities in Higher Education 2001–2002: Nineteenth Annual Status Report.* Washington D.C.: American Council on Education, 2002.

Hayes, E., and Colin III, S. (eds.). *Confronting Racism and Sexism.* New Directions for Adult and Continuing Education, no. 61. San Francisco: Jossey-Bass, 1994.

Hiemstra, R. (ed.). Creating Environments for Effective Adult Learning. New Directions for Adult and Continuing Education, no. 50. San Francisco: Jossey-Bass, 1991.

Holland, J. *The Relationship Between African-American Doctoral Students and Their Major.* 1993. (ED 359 915). [Available from http://md1.csa.com/csa/factsheets/eric.shtml.]

Hugo, J. M. "Adult Education History and the Issue of Gender: Toward a Different History of Adult Education in America." *Adult Education Quarterly,* 1990, *41*(1), 3–10.

Jackson, K. "Factors Associated with Alienation Among Black Faculty in Research." *Race and Ethnic Relations,* 1991, *6,* 123–144.

Jensen, G., Liveright, A., and Hallenbeck W. (eds.). *Adult Education: Outlines of an Emerging Field of University Study.* Washington D.C.: Adult Education Association of the U.S.A., 1964.

Lindeman, E. *The Meaning of Adult Education.* Montreal, Quebec: Harvest House, 1926.

Lorde, A. "There Is No Hierarchy of Oppression." In V. Cyrus (ed.), *Experiencing Race, Class and Gender in the United States.* (3rd ed.) Mountain View, Calif.: Mayfield Press, 2000.

Manglitz, E. "Challenging White Privilege in Adult Education." *Adult Education Quarterly,* 2003, *53*(2), 119–134.

Manning, M. *Dispatch from the Ebony Tower.* New York: Columbia University Press, 2000.

McIntosh, B. "White Privilege: Unpacking the Invisible Knapsack." In V. Cyrus (ed.),

Experiencing Race, Class and Gender in the United States. (3rd ed.) Mountain View, Calif.: Mayfield Press, 2000.

Mezirow, J. "Perspective Transformation." *Adult Education,* 1978, *28,* 100–110.

Nelson, T. D. *The Psychology of Prejudice.* Needham Heights, Mass.: Allyn & Bacon, 2002.

Neufeldt, H., and McGee, L. *Education of the African American Adult: A Historical Overview.* New York: Greenwood Press, 1990.

Peters, J., and Jarvis, P. *Adult Educator: Evolution and Achievements in a Developing Field of Study.* San Francisco: Jossey-Bass, 1991.

Peterson, E. A. (ed.). *Freedom Road: Adult Education of African Americans.* Malabar, Fla.: Krieger, 1996.

Rich, A. *The Feminist Classroom.* New York: Basic Books, 1994.

Ross-Gordon, J. "Serving Culturally Diverse Populations: A Social Imperative for Adult Education." In J. M. Ross-Gordon, L. G. Martin, and D. B. Briscoe (eds.), *Serving Culturally Diverse Populations.* New Directions for Adult and Continuing Education, no. 48. San Francisco: Jossey-Bass, 1990.

Ross-Gordon, J. M. "Needed: A Multicultural Perspective for Adult Education Research." *Adult Education Quarterly,* 1991, *42*(1), 1–2.

Sheared, V., and Sissel, P. A. (eds.). *Making Space: Merging Theory and Practice in Adult Education.* New York: Bergin & Garvey, 2001.

Slater, B. "The Growing Gender Gap in Black Higher Education." *Journal of Blacks in Higher Education,* 1994, *3,* 52–59.

Smith, S. "The Experience of African American Faculty in Adult Education Graduate Programs." Unpublished doctoral dissertation, Department of Educational Leadership, Ball State University, 1995.

Sowell, T. *Ethnic America.* New York: Basic Books, 1981.

Spring, J. *Deculturalization and the Struggle for Equality.* New York: McGraw-Hill, 2001.

Steele, S. *Content of Our Character.* New York: Harper Perennial, 1990.

Sue, D. W., and Sue, D. *Counseling the Culturally Different.* (2nd ed.) Somerset, N.J.: Wiley-Interscience, 1990.

Tatum, B. D. *Why Are All the Black Kids Sitting Together in the Cafeteria? And Other Conversations About Race.* New York: Basic Books, 2003.

Taylor-Archer, M., and Smith, S. *Our Stories: The Experiences of Black Professionals on Predominantly White Campuses.* Cincinnati, Ohio: JDOTT, 2002.

Tisdell, E. "Interlocking Systems of Power, Privilege, and Oppression in Adult Higher Education Classes." *Adult Education Quarterly,* 1993, *43*(3), 203–226.

Turner, C.S.V., and Meyers, S. L. *Faculty of Color in Academe: Bittersweet Success.* Boston: Pearson Allyn & Bacon, 1999.

Watters, E. "Claude Steel Has a Score to Settle." *New York Times Magazine,* Sept. 17, 1995, pp. 45–47.

Way, P. "Alain Leroy Locke: More Than the First Black President of AAAE." *Journal of Adult Education,* 1992, *21*(1), 15–21.

Witt, S. *The Pursuit of Race and Gender Equity in American Academe.* New York: Praeger, 1990.

Yamato, G. "Something About the Subject Makes It Hard to Name." In V. Cyrus (ed.), *Experiencing Race, Class and Gender in the United States.* (3rd ed.) Mountain View, Calif.: Mayfield Press, 2000.

SHERWOOD SMITH *is an assistant professor in Integrated Professional Studies and director of the Center for Cultural Pluralism at the University of Vermont.*

7

This chapter explores the marginality of university-based degree-granting adult education programs and considers how both hopes and fears add to the discourse about the field's vitality.

Adult Education Departments in the Entrepreneurial Age

Paul J. Ilsley

Whether or not degree-granting adult education programs are marginalized within higher education is subject to interpretation, but such debates can lead to an important discussion about the future of such programs within university settings. The case for marginalization can be made in light of what we know about the demise of key adult education programs during the past few decades at such universities as UCLA, UC Berkeley, Chicago, and Syracuse. These programs were abandoned for varied and complex reasons, but their closing suggests that the programs were not valued enough within the specific institutions. Many other adult education programs are also marginalized, devalued, and at risk of elimination, in part due to unique features of a program that distinguish it from others within higher education. Thus, even strong adult education programs are in danger of elimination (Milton, Watkins, Studdard, and Burch, 2003).

Is *marginality* the most precise term to describe what happened to these programs? How should we view the status of adult education today? When we consider the current state of higher education, it might be more correct to say that any program area can be marginalized or at least subject to rigorous and even damning reviews, due to changing political climates, shifting university missions, and budgetary shortfalls. The truth is that degree programs in many other areas have been cut. Programs have fallen in such areas as library science, communications, nursing, philosophy, law, and many other fields of study and disciplines up and down the university chain. This raises the specter that marginalization is a threat to our survival, not only from the outside but also at times from within higher education.

Still, the uniqueness of adult education programs is not immediately evident and often has to be explained, thus placing us in precarious positions during times of review and budget cuts. It is important to understand why this is so, relative to the context of higher education. It might be helpful to consider what the uniqueness of adult education programs means for positionality and possibilities in the academy. Adult education programs are quite different from other programs of education and also from other programs of professional preparation, meaning that we must often interpret ourselves and justify our work. Much of what makes us unique is our strength. For example, other programs, such as P–12 (preschool through grade 12) degree-granting programs, are regulated through certification, standardization, and course tracking in ways that are uncommon to, even unseen in, adult education. We enjoy a broader sense of purpose, scope, and professionalism, and a more recognizable workplace, than do more specialized programs such as nursing, engineering, communications, or library science. Such restrictions and standardization would likely compromise the flexibility inherent in and vital to adult education programs. The very characteristics that define our programs and give them strength may also raise flags. Such flag-raising program features can include internationalism, globalism, curricular scope and flexibility, and workplace and student diversity. We demonstrate an unusual array of conceptual bases, programming, and format flexibility—features that can further strengthen our educational mission. This is especially true when we are compared with other graduate programs in education but also holds true when we are compared with most other professional programs.

With the entrepreneurial and competitive demands on higher education, strong programming may not even be enough. Recent trends have altered the ways in which all programs are assessed. Among the most important trends is that the mission of the academy has changed from the traditional liberal arts curriculum of twenty years ago to one of increased entrepreneurship and outcome accountability today (Bok, 2003). Even a cursory look at criteria for effective institutions of higher learning reveals the importance of alumni job status; the ability to raise funds from alumni, corporations, foundations, and other granting agencies; and profitable partnerships with a variety of public, private, and voluntary agencies. Universities are multimillion-dollar organizations, a few multibillion. As Collins (1991) forecasted, gradually and nearly imperceptibly the criteria for success have shifted to a new productivity model. The emphasis has moved away from one based on providing a forum for intellectualism and well-roundedness through science and the liberal arts toward a more corporate model that encourages outcome measures defined in terms of career potential and vocation preparation.

The percentage of public funding for state universities such as Northern Illinois University (NIU) is decreasing. In a commencement address to graduates in 1995, the president of NIU, John LaTourette, informed the audience that the university moved from being a "state institution" through the 1970s and part of the 1980s, to a "state-assisted institution" during the 1980s and part of the 1990s, to a "state-located" institution from the mid-1990s on. Levels of state funding to public institutions are eroding to the point that many institutions across the country are cutting programs or undermining research and instructional efforts. Coupled with the fact that legislators and other leaders do not commonly read or refer to university-generated research, higher education administrators increasingly have been called upon to justify our work, load, time, and outcomes. The various university budget rescissions have led to skyrocketing tuition and delimiting, even curtailment, of programs.

The rise of tuition limits the numbers of potential students to those who can afford it. The shift of mission can therefore be interpreted as an assault on the lower and lower-middle classes, as well as on marginalized populations. Some forecast wholesale curtailment of diversity initiatives or at least much more restricted programs. In a sense, we are now a part of the war on the lower classes as many find themselves locked out of public higher education. Adult education leaders have a responsibility to become involved in these trends as well (Bok, 2003).

With the new financial constraints, the current academic reward structure promotes the entrepreneurial spirit, especially grant awards that bring resources into the university, in addition to the standard triad of research, service, and teaching. As the workload for professors has increased, they have more difficulty finding the time to do research and writing. Professors are advised to buy back their time with outside dollars. Consulting, partnerships, special contract teaching loads with cohorts of students, and partnerships with a variety of institutions and agencies are now commonplace and well-negotiated features of a professorial contract. The traditional assessment methods for faculty (tenure, promotion, sabbatical leave requests, and pay raises) and programs (quality of theses and dissertations, number of publications, diversity of students, and graduation rates) have remained in place, even with the advent of new pressures to demonstrate the entrepreneurial spirit or to bring in outside grant money. Faculty members have more responsibilities and pressures to fill the classroom seats, and they face more ways to be assessed, seemingly from different paradigms—the academic and the corporate.

As for the criteria used to evaluate programs, they too may vary and conflict conceptually, depending on who is asking. A program can be rewarded for recruiting large numbers of diverse and nontraditional students, but at the same time it may be questioned regarding admission or graduation standards. As universities are asked to do more with less, new criteria for accountability are emerging.

What do these changes mean for programs of adult education? So long as the courses are filled, the alumni base strong, the grants abundant, the programming innovative, the research strong, and the student population diverse, there are no problems. Programs that meet these demands are less likely to be marginalized. But what program can fulfill all of these goals?

Arguing Our Existence

Fortunately, some of the strengths of adult education programs often match with university missions and are supported by the accreditation policies of higher-learning commissions and university administrations. Serious questions deserve our attention. What it means to be a stable program is a matter of highlighting strengths and anticipating, even addressing, our weaknesses. First, let's discuss the criticisms, then the strengths.

What Critics Say About Adult Education. The subject matter in adult education programs is not well respected in some quarters. Finding voice in review, policy, and personnel boards, the harshest critics believe that our work is process-oriented, not content-driven, and that our body of knowledge overlaps with those of other disciplines (Jarvis, 1992). Of course, this interpretation is not correct and ought to be reexamined, but a related criticism is that the field of adult education is insular. Although our ideas and theories overlap with those of other disciplines, our publications do not cross into the journals and thinking outside our field; nor do we often seek others' perspectives by including literature from the outside (Jarvis, 1992). Critics believe our gene pool is getting weak. There really is no defense to this criticism.

Additionally, some colleagues and administrators are unclear about where our boundaries and purposes begin and end. Not only is there diversity of roles and missions but also diversity of paradigms, making us even more difficult to understand, as few single programs possess multiple paradigms within their accepted literature and scope. Likewise, we typically honor all forms of research, though currently favoring qualitative and narrative research. And although critical theory and radicalism are under attack these days by social and political conservatives, adult education also can provide a forum for these ideas to develop, indeed for all points of view to be expressed. Some of our colleagues, perhaps mostly from such fields as business, are suspicious of this mix of ideas and perspectives. However, other colleagues find our acceptance of myriad points of view refreshing and important.

At NIU as elsewhere, the adult education program emphasizes social responsibility through cultivation of professional mission. Many programs, in fact, integrate a mission of social justice with specific areas such as human resources development and continuing professional education. But criticisms of this focus have gotten louder, claiming programs are out of step with the times or appear to be antiadministration. Some programs are able to accept the criticisms, but others are forced to draw a conservative line and remain on the right side of it. Our challenge is to find a way to make social responsibility valued; otherwise, strong social stances will be discouraged, or worse, our well-being may well be jeopardized (Giroux, 1987).

What Gives Adult Education Strength on Campus. There is no substitute for involvement and action when one seeks platforms of power and influence. When professors of adult education assume leadership roles on campus and use their expertise in learning and teaching as a position to collaborate and consult with other leaders on campus, the programs are undoubtedly safer. This is certainly true at NIU, Georgia, Colorado, and Wyoming, as well as many other places where adult education faculty have worked at high levels of university administration. In places where faculty governance still matters, it is especially beneficial for adult education professors to be part of decision making, not only within the university but also in the professions. Certainly, it is also optimal when adult education faculty and students are involved with the processes that are common aspects of our field, such as designing continuing education programs, forging partnerships with institutions examining their learning needs, designing Web-based programs, advising diversity initiatives, or formulating innovative international learning opportunities. Although campus involvement, especially faculty governance opportunities, detracts from writing and from engagement with professional obligations, for a marginal field of study like ours, the effort is important. Through our involvement and presence at the table, we are able to educate others about our work and to cite our strengths and advantages—an imperative during times of austerity.

Still, regardless of leadership opportunities, there are also substantive claims that justify our work. The following list represents such claims.

Market-Force Advantages. Adult education programs, with the diversity of students and contacts, can reach marginalized groups as well as high-level policymakers seeking doctoral degrees. Adult education professors and staff have been among the first to create and implement innovative and flexible programs, such as weekend instruction, cohort programming, or guided independent study, in order to reach different populations. Furthermore, diverse alumni can advise and support the program—and the university as a whole. As higher education institutions adopt lifelong learning as a centerpiece of their missions, adult education programs can leverage their experience serving nontraditional populations and thus can connect with their universities' central missions (Clark, 1968).

Diversity. Student and faculty diversity are central to the missions of both higher and adult education. Thus, we can lend a valuable perspective when budget or other decisions necessitate trimming or redesigning diversity programs. Most programs of adult education have integrated the perspectives of marginalized groups into the classroom, curriculum, and research efforts. This can only bode well for us. Students of adult education come from many backgrounds and fields of practice, and our graduates take positions in a wider variety of workplaces than do graduates of many other university-based programs. This is an asset because when an alumni base is strong, so is the program's voice within the university.

Emphasis on Investigation and Practice of Learning Processes. All roads of adult education research lead to some aspect of learning. It is a safe and credible topic within the academy, and it augments the curriculum and professional development opportunities for other faculty very well. At NIU course topics include adult learning, program planning, human resource development, adult literacy and English as a second language, learning how to learn, continuing professional education, program planning, and multidisciplinary research approaches. Most of these topics support the status quo, as students learn skills that assist them in their work contexts. But new social agendas have changed adult education programs (Galbraith and Gilley, 1985); and this is the case at NIU, which emphasizes race, class, and gender studies. Consequently, internationalism, feminism, future studies, afrocentrism, and social movement studies are examples of course or research areas that are also emphasized at NIU for the purpose of expanding students' social visions. It is beneficial to explain this curriculum set to others, to stake our claim in these areas, or at least to be understood in terms of definable content.

Thought Actions That Protect the Margins of Adult Education

What about the future of adult education? It is one thing to protect our current interests, as suggested earlier, and quite another to be prepared to face challenges in the future. The assumption is made that any program can be slated for elimination and that no one is immune to critical review, a situation that demands vigilance and a watchful eye toward trends in higher education. As the mission of the university changes, leaders in adult education must understand the extent to which our goals and purposes support those changes in ways that do not undermine our own professional and social purposes. We also must recognize where the limits of compromise reside and when to resist the changes that impinge on our mission. To expand that thinking, the author offers the following recommendations in a spirit of holding true to the basic tenets of adult education, such as creating democratic programming, valuing individual experience, providing global discourses, and incorporating many knowledge bases into our curriculum (Vandenberg, 2000). Of course, the list can be expanded. The items have to do with principled beliefs regarding our own center. They each promote the ideal of expanding the definition of competence beyond discrete technical skills; and they raise further the extent to which the field should engage in discourse on ethical issues such as diversity, human rights, and sovereignty. To some the recommendations represent the very reason we face marginalization. To others they define who we are and give us the strength, which leads to the resources, we need. In other words, these recommendations emphasize our field's key principles, regardless of the results of marginalization.

- *Keep the focus on learning.* Adult education has a rightful place in advancing the topic of adult learning, including its psychological and sociological aspects. The key to success is ensuring that everyone knows the stake we claim along these lines. Announcing our accomplishments, conducting public lectures, and hosting conferences are a few ways to communicate our purpose. A fruitful idea is to invite people from various disciplines to collaborate with us (Ravitch and Viteritti, 2001).

- *Embrace diversity as a guiding vision to explain ourselves and to improve the academy.* The shape of society is changing rapidly (Bowen and Bok, 2000). Adult education can be a guiding light to ensure that the academy remains responsive to these changes, that marginalizing practices are minimized and inclusive practices maintained. Adult education can use its position at the margins to draw disparate voices together to create social conversations. Within our international mission, it behooves us to create experiences and opportunities for graduate students to witness global dialogues and to contribute to them.

- *Understand praxis, conscientization, and the sociopolitical purposes of education.* Adult educators know that education involves the brokering of power and that elitism is not the only way of approaching educational programming (Birzea, 1996; Bauman, 1998). Especially when finding spaces for historically marginalized groups, adult educators understand how a person gains voice, develops a consciousness about the world's politics, and learns to act. Advancing this view with the academy's decision makers is part of our mission.

- *Practice participatory and anticipatory politics.* Adult educators value participation and will expect it when warranted, despite practical concerns surrounding the central tendencies of technical rationality, such as efficiency, expertise, and standards (Engeström, 1987). Standards have their place but only to a point. Adopting an anticipatory stance would allow the adult education field to take a long-range view of the world and of our times. Therefore, we can meet challenges proactively, not reactively, by expanding social forums and tools for citizenship and world making (Niemi, 1999; Niemi and Ruohotie, 2002).

- *Maintain a focus on social visions and quality-of-life issues.* As the futurists remind us, the world is becoming increasingly less familiar (Cole, 1988). New configurations of nations, new confluences of power, and national and international conflicts dominate the landscape. It is highly desirable that we learn our way out of conflict toward prospects of peace and hope (McIntyre-Mills, 2000). Our hope is determined by our ability to envision a better world. This requires deliberate discussion and envisioning a better future. What issues can unite all adult educators, indeed all higher educators, better than quality-of-life issues? Adult education programs are ideally suited to take a leadership role within international discourses on what quality of life means and what our role is in obtaining it.

- *Realize the potential for educators in offering both the liberal and democratic social forums.* The methods for creating social forums abound and can be found in the time-honored Nordic traditions of the folk school and the study circle. With an expanded set of skills for providing forums, educators will be in a position to promote democracy, consensus, and grassroots community values.

In part due to our marginalized status, adult educators are well suited to transcend boundaries of different social worlds. How can we use this opportunity to facilitate understanding of what higher education can achieve? At the same time, how can we contribute to the global discourse on what it means to be educated? We are called to bring to the fore discussions on diversity, justice, liberty, equality, and peace. Without our convictions intact, perhaps the best we can do is cling to the wreckage. But with conviction and savvy, we ensure our place within the academy.

References

Bauman, Z. *Globalization: The Human Consequences.* Oxford: Polity Press, 1998.

Birzea, C. *Education for Democratic Citizenship.* Strasbourg: Council of Europe, 1996.

Bok, D. *Universities in the Marketplace: The Commercialization of Higher Education.* Princeton, N.J.: Princeton University Press, 2003.

Bowen, W. G., and Bok, D. *The Shape of the River: Long-Term Consequences of Considering Race in College and University Admissions.* (2nd ed.) Princeton, N.J.: Princeton University Press, 2000.

Clark, B. *Adult Education in Transition: A Study of Institutional Insecurity.* Berkeley: University of California Press, 1968.

Cole, M. "Cross-Cultural Research in the Sociohistorical Tradition." *Human Development,* 1988, *31,* 137–151.

Collins, M. *Adult Education as Vocation: A Critical Role for the Adult Educator.* New York: Routledge, 1991.

Engeström, Y. *Learning by Expanding: An Activity-Theoretical Approach to Developmental Research.* Helsinki: Orienta-Konsultit, 1987.

Galbraith, M. W., and Gilley, J. W. "An Examination of Professional Certification." *Lifelong Learning,* 1985, *11*(2), 15, 18.

Giroux, H. A. "Citizenship, Public Philosophy, and the Struggle for Democracy." *Educational Theory,* 1987, *37*(2), 103–120.

Jarvis, P. "Leaders of Adult and Continuing Education Should Come from Outside the Field." In R. G. Brockett and M. W. Galbraith (eds.), *Confronting Controversies in Challenging Times: A Call for Action.* New Directions for Adult and Continuing Education, no. 54. San Francisco: Jossey-Bass, 1992.

LaTourette, J. President's address, graduate school commencement exercises, Northern Illinois University, May 13, 1995.

McIntyre-Mills, J. J. *Global Citizenship and Social Movements.* Amsterdam: Harwood Academic Publishers, 2000.

Milton, J., Watkins, K. E., Studdard, S. S., and Burch, M. "The Ever Widening Gyre: Factors Affecting Change in Adult Education Graduate Programs in the United States." *Adult Education Quarterly,* 2003, *54*(1), 23–41.

Niemi, H. (ed.). *Moving Horizons in Education: International Transformations and Challenges of Democracy.* Helsinki: University of Helsinki Press, 1999.

Niemi, H., and Ruohotie, P. *Theoretical Understandings for Learning in the Virtual University*. Helsinki: University of Helsinki Press, 2002.

Ravitch, D., and Viteritti, J. P. (eds.). *Making Good Citizens: Education and Civil Society*. New Haven, Conn.: Yale University Press, 2001.

Vandenberg, A. *Citizenship and Democracy in a Global Era*. New York: St. Martin's Press, 2000.

PAUL J. ILSLEY *is a professor of Educational Research and Adult Education, Northern Illinois University, and docent in Adult Education at the University of Helsinki.*

8

This chapter uses a case study of an interdisciplinary online adult health education (eHealth) research program to address how adult education can survive and thrive in research universities.

At the Margins of the Research Enterprise: Learning from an Interdisciplinary eHealth Research Program

Meg Wise, Betta Owens

This chapter joins a growing dialogue about factors that marginalize academic departments of adult education (Imel, Brockett, and James, 2000; Milton, Watkins, Studdard, and Burch, 2003). We will address two factors. First, pressure is increasing to garner extramural research funding. And second, other fields have taken the research lead on profound and complex adult-lifespan learning issues, such as chronic or life-threatening health conditions. To illustrate these issues, we will describe an interdisciplinary Web-based adult patient education (eHealth) research program in which we have worked for more than a decade. We will conclude with a discussion of implications for adult education research.

The Ascending Research Enterprise

Over the past decades, research has come to trump teaching and community service, especially in Research I universities, whose primary focus is on advanced graduate studies and research (Bok, 2003). Although garnering generous extramural funding cannot fully inoculate against threats of departmental consolidation, reduction, or closure, it is increasingly required for survival. Adult education is at a disadvantage because most (but not all) high-dollar extramural research awards go to scientific study designs with large samples that show promise for building coherent research programs. Some argue quite cogently that as a practitioner-oriented field, adult education should not invest undue energy toward building self-sustaining research programs, because doing so would dilute the primary purpose of our research, which is to support teaching, learning, and service in particular settings (Collins, 1992). However, in the entrepreneurial paradigm, prolific grant getters are rewarded; the not-so-prolific are marginalized. The reasons are straightforward. Universities rely on grant overhead to cover general operations (for example, libraries, liberal arts teaching) in the face of diminishing tax support and rising costs. Moreover, funding for innovative and high-profile research brings enormous prestige, which in turn attracts talented students, faculty, and private donations. Adult education (and other education departments) may be more at risk than applied fields with robust and well-funded research components, such as engineering, psychology, nursing, and medicine. The social forces that contribute to lower levels of research funding for adult education are immense and complex. However, we suggest that with the confluence of (1) increasing awareness that learning in the face of illness requires a holistic approach and (2) increasing funding for integrative social science-based adult health education, the time is ripe for adult education to collaborate on interdisciplinary patient education research.

The Expanding Margins of Adult Health Education Research

Traditionally, patient education has used rational, behavioral, and deficit learning models to help individuals achieve measurable outcomes based on educator rather than learner-defined goals. For example, cardiac rehabilitation programs focus more on the mechanical (learning to measure blood pressure) and behavioral (exercise training or dietary change) aspects of managing illness than on the emotional, social, and spiritual aspects of learning to be whole in the face of limitations (Ornish, 1998; Wise, 2001, 2003). But such approaches often fail to yield preset bio-behavioral outcomes especially for non-Western or low-income patients or for those with unresolved emotional and relationship issues (Daaleman and Vandecreek, 2000). There is a growing awareness that health crises are universal events in the adult lifespan. Albeit unwanted and uninvited, they pose opportunities for profound learning in technical, social, behavioral, and existential realms. Some clinics have integrated non-Western medicine and practices that enhance personal reflection and transformation (Kleinman, 1998; Ornish, 1998).

Rsearch funding has been steadily increasing for eHealth patient education programs that can expand access to such innovations. This is likely to continue given trends toward managed healthcare cost containment and graying baby boomers' use of the Internet, patient advocacy, and mind-body medicine. eHealth research addresses how people construct the meaning of health and illness, the locus of decision making; how technology can be used for cognitive and psychosocial learning; and how the digital divide can be reduced (Gustafson and others, 2001). Adult educators have not traditionally designed or evaluated patient education, but these expanded margins of the health and eHealth fields intersect with adult education's theories and mission and thus provide new opportunities for collaboration.

The Comprehensive Health Enhancement Support System (CHESS)

Housed in a self-supporting interdisciplinary research center at the University of Wisconsin–Madison, CHESS (http://chess.chsra.wisc.edu/Chess/) was started in 1990 by David Gustafson, a professor of industrial engineering and preventive medicine, to help people live better with a serious health condition (Gustafson and others, 1993). He hypothesized that patients knowledgeable about their illness, treatment options, and the healthcare system could get better care, be proactive and positive in the face of challenge, equalize the power asymmetry between doctors and patients, and ultimately influence quality improvements in health care delivery systems.

CHESS has since developed, evaluated, and continuously enhanced eHealth programs to empower people living with the challenges of cancer, HIV/AIDS, heart disease, asthma, and other conditions. CHESS delivers in-home, 24/7, confidential access to information, peer and expert support, and interactive skill-building activities to help people live well in the face of health crises and become full partners in their treatment decisions and self-care (Gustafson and others, 1993, 2001). Program development is driven by the needs and struggles of people living with the illness and inspired by their resilience. Patients' needs are discerned through an extensive process, including literature reviews, focus groups, in-depth qualitative interviews, survey questionnaires, and ongoing field research (Boberg and others, 2003). Randomized evaluation studies suggest that CHESS improves people's quality of life and participation in health care and that it reduces use of expensive health care services (Gustafson and others, 2001). Secondary data analyses augmented by in-depth interviews, detailed logs of CHESS use, and online support-group texts have explored how CHESS fits into the existential aspects of living with the illness and how use patterns affect quality of life and other outcomes (Smaglik and others, 1998; Shaw and others, 2000; Wise, Yun, and Shaw, 2000; Wise, 2001, 2003).

Convergence of CHESS with Adult Education Theories. CHESS's operating assumptions overlap with the well-articulated adult education theories of transformative learning and self-directed learning.

Transformative and Other Learning Theories. CHESS's underlying assumption is that a serious illness is a disorienting dilemma that can motivate people to make new meaning of their life (perspective transformation), to learn about the technical and psychosocial aspects of the illness, and to realign actions with reframed priorities. CHESS is also informed by self-efficacy theory (Gustafson and others, 1993), which suggests a range of cognitive and social activities, such as self-monitoring, information, coaching, role models, social support, reflective trial and error, and narrative life review. To that end, CHESS provides information in a range of formats, tools to construct knowledge and meaning (for example, online peer support groups, personal stories, and journaling), interactive planning and decision-making tools, and self-guided cognitive behavior therapy exercises.

An Evolving Self-Directed Learning System. Originally, CHESS assumed a completely self-directed learner, choosing (or not) to log in, to participate in online support groups, or to search for salient materials. Later CHESS added more complex dimensions of self-directed learning by building algorithms to provide automatic prompts, self-assessments, and tailored messages with links. More recently it has integrated a monthly educational phone call from an asthma nurse to help learners control their asthma symptoms and to recommend salient CHESS learning activities. The nurse manages these phone calls with a toolbox that displays the learner's biweekly report of symptoms, asthma management activities, and quality of life, as well as a "prescription pad" to recommend CHESS activities that appear on the learner's home page. Between calls the nurse is available by secured internal e-mail.

Digital Divide and Health Disparities. CHESS is committed to reducing the digital divide through research and mentoring minority scholars. Research funds provide a computer, Internet access, phone lines, training, and technical support, as needed (Gustafson and others, 2001). The Digital Divide Pilot Project, with support from the National Cancer Institute and the Markle Foundation, offered CHESS to any woman with breast cancer living within 250 percent of the poverty line in one inner-city community and one rural region. It resulted in more effective recruitment, training, and dissemination processes.

Interdisciplinary Teamwork for Multiple Perspectives. The CHESS team represents a range of disciplines and perspectives to address the learning needs of the whole person facing the multiple challenges of living with an illness. These include faculty from engineering, medicine, nursing, communications, psychology, as well as doctorate- and master's-level staff from library science, adult education, social marketing, school psychology, social work, and computer and graphic design. Statisticians, qualitative research methodologists, and specialists (for example, oncologists, cardiologists) consult on data analysis and interpretation as well as on content development. Research partners have included a variety of healthcare and academic organizations in the United States and Canada. Thus, eHealth is a dynamic field of basic and applied research across several disciplines. It attracts innovative and creative thinkers—natural boundary spanners who are grounded in their own discipline and can embrace the perspectives of others to build an integrated theory and practice. Although adult education perspectives are represented at CHESS, they are not cited in the otherwise interdisciplinary eHealth literature. Conversely, a scan of the education databases indicates that the adult education literature does not cite the vast literature related to learning in the face of illness from psychology, nursing, or other health-related fields.

Funding a Self-Sustaining Research Program. CHESS, like many other research projects, has relied on soft money since its inception. It was originally funded by a grant from the W. K. Kellogg Foundation and subsequently by grants from the National Institutes of Health and nonprofit foundations. Studies address both outcome and process research questions and develop new features, such as increasing capabilities to personalize or tailor the learning online session, reaching out to the patients' social network, and integrating a human coach.

Building a research program (versus isolated research projects) entails holding some aims and measures constant while continuously forging new questions and methods. For example, CHESS has used the same measures for health information, proficiency, participation and satisfaction with treatment decisions, and quality of life across studies. For instance, a current asthma study is expanding the research scope by mapping the links between new learning processes (such as information competence, overcoming psychosocial barriers, and setting salient goals), asthma self-management (such as taking medications and avoiding asthma triggers), and health and quality of life outcomes (such as fewer symptoms, lost days from school or work, and greater participation in enjoyable activities).

In addition, a Center of Excellence in Cancer Communication Research grant for program development, basic and applied research, and training scholars in eHealth will extend CHESS beyond the individual cancer patient to his or her social support network. It will assess reducing the burden on caregiver and partner-patient and physician communication; and it will explore how people discover, enhance, and develop their psychosocial assets in the face of living with advanced cancer.

Sustaining a research enterprise is an enormous collaborative effort involving the interdisciplinary research team, recruitment sites, and support staff. Nabbing a highly competitive award requires—over and above an innovative idea and solid research methodology—an impressive track record and the home institution's support. Thus, staff can devote several months per year to writing grants and publishing results in peer-reviewed journals.

Implications for Adult Education

This example illustrates how scholars collaborate across disciplines in a self-sustaining eHealth research program whose mission and learning theories converge with those of adult education. It also shows that establishing and sustaining a program of innovative research and development takes on a life of its own. So what lessons can adult education programs take from this example if they are to survive and thrive in entrepreneurial research environments? And what does it mean that adult education, as a field of research, is not centrally involved in these research programs that develop and evaluate comprehensive, innovative adult-lifespan learning programs?

First, let us consider whether the costs to play the high-stakes research game diminish adult education's mission to support teaching and service. If this is so, the field might indeed be better served by ceding its place at Research I institutions, as has been the trend in recent years (Milton, Watkins, Studdard, and Burch, 2003). However, we find it instructive to reflect on Houle's three-tiered pyramid (1956), in which adult education professors, the smallest tier, train and support adult education practitioners, the middle tier (see Editors' Notes and Knox, Chapter Two, this volume).

Notably, since Houle articulated this model, extramural research has trumped teaching and service and risen to the top of the academic triumvirate. In this scenario innovative collaborative research expands disciplinary margins and creative frontiers within academic and scientific power structures. Thus, as we revisit Houle's pyramid (1956) nearly a half a century later—in light of adult education's increased professionalization, research orientation, and theory development—we suggest that the field can survive and thrive in the research enterprise through more strategic interdisciplinary research collaboration. We believe this endeavor will better support field practitioners while it advances knowledge of adult-lifespan learning from multiple disciplinary perspectives.

Let's examine adult education's relative absence from the dialogue about holistic learning in the face of illness and about eHealth research and development. We have identified four factors. First, funding agencies typically favor hypothesis-driven research that test sample-wide effects on educational interventions, but adult educators more often focus on individual learning processes and experiences within educational interventions. Second, adult education graduate training produces more qualitative than quantitative researchers, but qualitative research is often perceived to lack the rigor. Third, concepts of adult development and lifelong learning are now widely accepted and operationalized across popular, business, and academic cultures. Fourth and finally, adult education's theories and core knowledge base borrow heavily from psychology, sociology, and other disciplines, while its process components, such as program planning leadership and collaboration, are shared by several fields. Given these factors, the perception may be that adult education does not bring a sufficiently unique body of knowledge or theory to an innovative interdisciplinary team of boundary spanners (Wise and Glowacki-Dudka, 2003).

Nonetheless, we believe that eHealth stands to benefit from adult education's well-articulated body of research-based theory and practice, its commitment to learner-defined agendas, and its fluid integration of multiple and polar perspectives (the silver lining of eclecticism). Learning to live with a life-limiting health condition is a continuous dialogue between the sociological and psychological, behavioral and constructivist, critical and humanistic, deficit and asset. In addition to the transformative and self-directed learning theories discussed earlier, we believe that adult education's most valuable contribution to interdisciplinary adult eHealth education may be its assets-focused learning and experience-focused evaluation. Meanwhile, critical social theory can illuminate the limits of working within the margins of respectability—a factor that stops many mainstream interventions from helping people to critically evaluate, organize, and change the embedded social artifacts of poverty-induced illness.

Assets-Focused Learning and Meaning Making

Health disciplines such as medicine, nursing, and psychology now espouse patient- or client-centered and assets-focused philosophies. However, traditionally steeped in expert-driven approaches based on deficit models, these disciplines are less seasoned than adult education at eliciting and integrating people's assets, the meaning they find in the illness experience, the goals they choose, and the actions they take. Moreover, program development, guided by proving a study's hypothesized outcomes, tips the control of the learning agenda (albeit respectfully) more toward expert-defined goals (for example, adopting a low-fat diet) than toward helping people choose learning goals based on their evolving understanding of the experience (for example, relationships as life purpose).

Finally, coming from a paradigm of problem solving and quality improvement, formative exploratory research focuses on assessing people's needs without assessing the assets they brought to the illness, the strategies they used to develop or apply them to cope with the experience, or the way they have learned and grown through the process. Thus, the health disciplines may give more attention to using a narrow evidence-based bio-behavioral regimen to control a chronic illness than to providing guidance for reflective meaning making or identifying and enhancing one's assets to meet the illness challenge—which may be the well of inspiration to adopt a disease-management regimen (Ornish, 1998; Wise, 2003). Certainly, as Courtenay, Merriam, Reeves, and Baumgartner (2000) have demonstrated, adult education's fierce commitment to and considerable research and experience in understanding, eliciting, and facilitating authentic learner-focused agendas is a significant voice in understanding learning through the illness experience and would be a great contribution to eHealth collaborative research.

Experience and Process-Focused Evaluation. Large-scale research evaluates significant samplewide effects of eHealth programs, whereas adult education research more often evaluates the individuals' learning experience within and outside a formal education program. Both approaches are valuable and more so when they work hand in hand. System-level evaluations often use mediational models to measure how process variables affect learning outcomes, which scholars identify a priori from the theory and research literature. For instance, CHESS's randomized heart disease study measured the learning outcome of adopting a low-fat diet mediated by increasing diet self-efficacy (as measured by perceived knowledge, social support for diet, and diet actions and attitudes). However, a qualitative study of individual learning experiences found that a low-fat diet was often not the learner's goal (Wise, 2003). Instead, people reported that sharing fears and a deepened sense of purpose online and seeing that others with even more serious illness could carry on with grace and humor helped them make meaning of their heart attack; the meaning participants ascribed to the experience and their lives was a key factor in their adopting healthy lifestyles. Meaning making was neither an outcome nor a mediator measure for the quantitative component of the evaluation.

Critical Theories: Acknowledging the Margins of Funded Research. Pedagogical approaches for funded eHealth studies use humanistic and social-cognitive adult learning theories that help individuals identify their needs and develop the proficiency to face them. However, these approaches do not support critical social theories that help people reflect on and organize to change the underlying social conditions and power relationships that disadvantage them. For instance, CHESS empowers people to take individual actions and responsibility for their health and self-care. An individual action to control asthma can include monitoring air pollution and staying inside on high-pollution days. But to our knowledge, federally funded patient education Web sites encourage neither the critical analysis of federal policies that have relaxed carbon dioxide emission standards, nor direct citizen action to challenge such policies. Likewise, eHealth sites provide information about free medication programs, but do not help people evaluate the effects of legislation that shields pharmaceutical companies from lower-priced imported medicines or group-negotiated bulk rates. Finally, these sites do not help people analyze the power relations underlying these policies and legislation, nor specific road maps to circumvent them (such as links to Web sites to order prescription medications from Canada). Thus, federally funded research bumps up against the margins of power and must cede deeper-level social justice activism to other change agents—outside such funding structures.

Rigor and Stereoscopic Vision. Finally, we must take seriously the perception that adult education lacks rigor. Like Cervero (1992), we hope that we would focus as much on outcomes as on process. Specifically, we must embrace a stereoscopic and holistic perspective of integrative research methods and reconsider a tendency toward parochial demonizing of hard outcomes and theory-driven hypothesis testing. The National Institutes of Health increasingly support qualitative research with clear and cogent rationale for sample selection, interview questions, analysis methodology, data-supported findings and interpretations, and suggestions for how the research will advance further understanding. Advanced graduate training should thus require familiarity with research literatures of related disciplines, proficiency in writing grant proposals, and cross-method research design.

This example of a funded eHealth research program suggests that adult education faculty should vigorously collaborate with researchers in and outside of the school of education who address adult-lifespan learning issues from technical, psychosocial, spiritual, and narrative perspectives. This will allow today's and tomorrow's adult education scholars to push the margins of understanding and to facilitate holistic adult education principles across a wider range of challenging health and life events.

Conclusion

Adult education sits at the threatened margins of universities that increasingly reward self-supporting research programs. Whereas educational research has been the poor stepsister of the better-endowed health-related research fields, funding for interdisciplinary eHealth research is growing in the face of recognition that people need a range of educational strategies to manage the technical, behavioral, and existential aspects of living with inevitable health problems. Adult education does not typically collaborate in eHealth research despite shared mission, theories, and assumptions about the potential for transformative learning in the face of a major illness. However, we believe adult education's well-articulated body of research and practice can and should inform interdisciplinary eHealth research.

In contemplating such collaborations, we suggest that the field examine its biases against fully integrating outcomes with process-oriented research—while encouraging critical change agents to push the margins of mainstream research. We further suggest that demonstrated proficiency in grant writing and interdisciplinary research design be required for advanced graduate training. Finally, we suggest that a fourth component might be added to Houle's 1956 paradigm: the academic staff researcher who collaborates fluidly with faculty, students, learners, and their communities.

References

Boberg, E., and others. "Assessing the Unmet Information, Support, and Care Delivery Needs of Men with Prostate Cancer." *Patient Education and Counseling,* 2003, *49*(3), 233–242.

Bok, D. *Universities in the Marketplace: The Commercialization of Higher Education.* Princeton, N.J.: Princeton University Press, 2003.

Cervero, R. M. "Adult and Continuing Education Should Strive for Professionalization." In R. G. Brockett and M. W. Galbraith (eds.), *Confronting Controversies in Challenging Times: A Call for Action.* New Directions for Adult and Continuing Education, no. 54. San Francisco: Jossey-Bass, 1992.

Collins, M. "Adult and Continuing Education Should Resist Further Professionalization." In R. G. Brockett and M. W. Galbraith (eds.), *Confronting Controversies in Challenging Times: A Call for Action.* New Directions for Adult and Continuing Education, no. 54. San Francisco: Jossey-Bass, 1992.

Courtenay, B., Merriam, S., Reeves, P., and Baumgartner, L. "Perspective Transformation over Time: A Two-Year Follow-up Study of HIV-Positive Adults." *Adult Educational Quarterly,* 2002, *50*(2), 102–115.

Daaleman, T., and VandeCreek, L. "Placing Religion and Spirituality in End-of-Life Care." *JAMA,* 2000, *284*(19), 2514–2517.

Gustafson, D., and others. "Development and Pilot Evaluation of a Computer-Based Support System for Women with Breast Cancer." *Journal of Psychosocial Oncology,* 1993, *11*(4), 69–93.

Gustafson, D., and others. "CHESS: Ten Years of Research and Development in Consumer Health Informatics for Broad Populations, Including Underserved." *International Journal of Medical Informatics,* 2001, *65,* 169–177.

Houle, C. "The Development of Leadership." Chap. 4 in *Liberal Adult Education.* White Plains, N.Y.: Fund for Adult Education, 1956.

Imel, S., Brockett, R. G., and James, W. B. "Defining the Profession: A Critical Appraisal." In E. Hayes and A. Wilson (eds.), *Handbook of Adult and Continuing Education.* San Francisco: Jossey-Bass, 2000.

Kleinman, A. *The Illness Narratives: Suffering, Healing, and the Human Condition.* New York: Basic Books, 1988.

Milton, J., Watkins, K. E., Studdard, S. S., and Burch, M. "The Ever Widening Gyre: Factors Affecting Change in Adult Education Graduate Programs in the United States." *Adult Education Quarterly,* 2003, *54*(1), 23–41.

Ornish, D. *Love and Survival.* New York: HarperCollins, 1998.

Shaw, B., and others. "Experiences of Women with Breast Cancer: Exchanging Social Support over the CHESS Computer Network." *Journal of Health Communication,* 2000, *5*(2), 135–159.

Smaglik, P., and others. "The Quality of Interactive Computer Use Among HIV-Infected Individuals." *Journal of Health Communication,* 1998, 3(1), 39–54.

Wise, M. "Expanding the Limits of Evidence-Based Medicine: A Discourse Analysis of Cardiac Rehabilitation Clinical Practice Guidelines." Paper presented at the 42nd Adult Education Research Conference, East Lansing, Michigan, June 2001.

Wise, M. "Balancing Assets and Deficits: Who Controls the Online Patient Education Learning Agenda?" Paper presented at the 44th annual Adult Education Research Conference, San Francisco, Calif., June 2003.

Wise, M., and Glowacki-Dudka, M. "Working with Interdisciplinary Teams of Boundary Spanners: The Challenges and Potential for Adult Education." Paper presented at the 22nd Annual Midwest Research-to-Practice Conference in Adult, Continuing and Community Education, Columbus, Ohio, Oct. 2003.

Wise, M., Yun, G. W., and Shaw, B. "Mapping Use of a Self-Directed On-line Heart Disease Education Program onto Health Learning Outcomes: A Study of Post–Heart Attack Learners." Paper presented at the 41st annual Adult Education Research Conference, Vancouver, British Columbia, June 2000.

MEG WISE *is an assistant scientist for the CHESS project at the Center for Health Systems Research and Analysis, University of Wisconsin–Madison.*

BETTA OWENS *is a researcher at the Center for Health Systems Research and Analysis, University of Wisconsin–Madison.*

This chapter discusses multiple challenges and pathways to address the margins of adult education and poses question for future consideration.

9

Embracing and Expanding the Margins of Adult Education

Meg Wise, Michelle Glowacki-Dudka

The chapters in this volume have addressed several challenges, opportunities, and accomplishments in adult education. These chapters articulate a common message that being on the margins, although frustrating, can foster creativity and transformation in the service of the social good. In the Editors' Notes, we brought up the notion of volition—that is, to a large extent adult educators choose to work at the margins. In their own way, the contributors described why and how they pushed the social boundaries that deny justice, health, and education to marginalized segments of the adult population.

It is not surprising that a volume about margins of a broad field like adult education will identify multiple definitions and pathways to address them. Knox's chapter, "From Margin to Mainstream to Collaboration," describes a theme that runs through many chapters. Collaboration—across the tiers of adult education, across social organizations, and across academic disciplines—can create a fluid interchange between margins and center. For instance, Charaniya and Walsh describe how their work for Islamic-Jewish interreligious dialogue, at the invisible margins of society and adult education, was catapulted to center stage after the September 11 attacks. Although Ilsley notes that even flourishing departments of adult education may feel pangs of marginality within the academy, they are the center of prestige and power within the field of adult education. As Knox succinctly noted, determining which is center and which is margin is a matter of perspective. However, we agree that the notion of margins contains the sense both of opportunity and of threat. In fact, numerous theories identify that the most transformative learning comes from a sense of a disorienting dilemma, a threat, or a crisis (Mezirow, 2000).

Maintaining a sense of mission and voice can be challenging and lonely for adult educators working in isolation with stretched resources and an institution's eye on the bottom-line deliverables. The purpose of this volume has been to provide positive examples of how adult educators can stretch margins, despite obvious barriers, for the betterment of society.

From this acknowledgment of struggle, we call out pathways to expand the boundaries of adult education by embracing the values that draw us to the margins. If the heart draws us to the margins, the hand and head (or the analysis and know-how) must be equal partners in the pathway to actualize our vision.

The metaphor introduced in the Editors' Notes of adult education as a mighty river reminds us that a wide and unruly river can be greater than the sum of its more defined disciplinary tributaries. However, navigating such a river and irrigating communities beyond the immediate floodplain that nurtures the complexities of adult life—family, work, spirituality, health, higher education, diversity, and social justice—requires that we be critically reflective, socially enlightened, competent, and flexible to the conditions we face.

For instance, Smith in Chapter Six and Ilsley in Chapter Seven struggled and negotiated with technocratic and bottom-line definitions of competence that serve dominant social and power structures and disenfranchise the margins. However, Knox in Chapter Two and Wise and Owens in Chapter Eight described how adult education can bring its understanding of margins to augment enlightened and innovative ideas that are generated at the center. Alternatively, the popular education approach described by Larson in Chapter Four builds strength at the margins without appealing to the power at the center.

In yet another set of conditions, Truty in Chapter Five and Smith in Chapter Six described the personal struggles that come with the contradictions inherent in representing the interests of power-poor groups from a quasi-insider position within organizational and social structures. After facilitating her colleagues' downsizing and then being downsized herself, Truty rejected the human resource development (HRD) role. However, at the close of her chapter she is wrestling with the possibility for HRD professionals to change power relations from within the corporate workplace—a change more typically associated with the solidarity of organized labor movements. Likewise, Smith is an African American faculty member who wrestles with his dual role of the privileged insider who is called upon to speak on behalf of minority students while simultaneously withstanding outsider status and its associated pejorative assumptions about his (and by definition all minority scholars') academic competence. Smith's chapter, however, leaves the reader with sense of a growing community of minority scholars, albeit at different institutions.

Assets and Challenges

To embrace and expand the margins of adult education, we must recognize and activate the full range of our assets, as described in this volume and elsewhere. However, we must also be mindful of the threats and limits (along with the freedoms) that can accompany life at the margins. For instance, as described in Chapter Three, the events of September 11, 2001, brought Charaniya into suspect status, due to membership in a marginalized group and perhaps to her visible work at the margins. While her story did not end in catastrophe, it reminds us that adult education can be subversive and dangerous (Freire, 1985, 1992; Giroux, 2001). Educators who challenge the margins of power—from labor organizing, civil rights and voter registration movements, and peace movements—have faced consequences (Horton and Freire, 1990). Although such examples now may seem extreme, each of us must define our relationships to professional and social margins. With that caveat, we end with some questions about more traditional notions of adult education's margins.

Questions for the Future

We conclude this volume with five questions to overcome threats and embrace the strengths encountered at the margins of adult education.

1. How can we identify, embrace, and enhance the power at the field's margins?
2. What is adult education's unique and core technical knowledge, and how is it valuable across the collaboration landscape?
3. How can adult educators include and serve underrepresented groups working for social justice?
4. How important is it for adult education to sit at the cutting edge of interdisciplinary research that addresses lifespan-learning issues (for example, workplace, health, literacy)?
5. How can we as adult educators broaden our research and scholarship scope to serve adult education practitioners and policymakers?

The Last Word

We leave the last word to Sheared and Sissel (2001, p. 328): "[We] ought to revel in that fact that it [adult education] is marginal."

References

Freire, P. *The Politics of Education: Culture, Power, and Liberation.* New York: Bergin & Garvey, 1985.

Freire, P. *Pedagogy of the Oppressed.* New York: Continuum, 1992.

Giroux, H. "Pedagogy of the Depressed: Beyond the New Politics of Cynicism." *College Literature,* 2001, 28(3), 1–32.

Horton, M., and Freire, P. *We Make the Road by Walking: Conversations on Education and Social Change.* Philadelphia: Temple University Press, 1990.

Mezirow, J., and associates. *Learning as Transformation: Critical Perspectives on a Theory in Progress.* San Francisco: Jossey-Bass, 2000.

Sheared, V., and Sissel, P. A. "What Does Research, Resistance, and Inclusion Mean for Adult Education Practice? A Reflective Response." In V. Sheared and P. A. Sissel (eds.), *Making Space: Merging Theory and Practice in Adult Education.* New York: Bergin & Garvey, 2001.

MEG WISE *is an assistant scientist for the CHESS project at the Center for Health Systems Research and Analysis, University of Wisconsin–Madison.*

MICHELLE GLOWACKI-DUDKA *is an assistant professor of Adult, Higher, and Community Education at Ball State University.*

INDEX

Action research, 26, 27
Addams, J., 39
Adult education: abandoning programs in, 67; criticisms of, 70–71; current trends in, 17; definition of, 7; future of, 72–74, 89; goals for, 11–12; historical foundation of, 7–9; historical trends in, 18; versus human resources development, 12; principles of, 39; as profession, 10–11; purpose of, 9; as social action, 11, 40–42; strengths of, 71–72; types of people enrolling in, 20; uniqueness of, 68
Adult Education and Family Literacy Act (AEFLA), 42
Adult education degrees, 8
Adult Education Quarterly, 58
Adult Education Research Conference, 9, 58
Adult educators: coordination among, 12; versus cultural creatives, 18; of emancipatory learning, 45–46; in Houle's three-tiered pyramid, 2, 8; number of, 12; role of, 8, 39–42
AEFLA. *See* Adult Education and Family Literacy Act (AEFLA)
African American faculty, 57–63. *See also* Professors
American Association for Adult and Continuing Education, 9, 26–27
American Association for Adult Education, 18
American Association of Community Colleges, 22
Anderson, S. R., 18
Apple, M., 11
Assets-focused learning, 83–85
Associations, 27
Authentic learning, 43–44

Banks, J., 58, 63
Bauman, Z., 73
Baumgartner, L., 83
Beder, H., 9
Behavior changes, 35
Bell, D., 60
Betrayal, 51, 52
Birzea, C., 73
Blackwell, J. E., 58

Blakely, R. J., 17, 18, 27
Boberg, E., 79
Bok, D., 68, 69, 73, 77
Bonner, F. A., 61
Boshier, R., 10
Bowen, W. G., 73
Boys, M., 29, 30
Boyte, H. C., 19, 26
Brabeck, M., 41
Brockett, R. G., 8, 9, 10, 13, 77
Brookfield, S., 39
Budget cuts, 67–69, 78
Burbules, N. C., 53
Burch, M., 8, 9–10, 67, 77, 82
Byndon, A., 59

Callister, T. A., 53
Cardiac rehabilitation programs, 78
Caron, P., 42, 43, 44
Carr, W., 61
Catholic Diocese of Columbus, 22
Center of Excellence in Cancer Communication Research grant, 81
Certification, 10
Cervero, R. M., 11, 12, 13, 29, 85
Charaniya, N. K., 4, 29, 30–31, 31–33, 34, 36, 87, 89
CHESS. *See* Comprehensive Health Enhancement Support System (CHESS)
CHIPPY. *See* Community Education Center and Home-based Instructional Program for Parents and Youth (CHIPPY)
Citizen Leadership Institute (CLI), 21–22
Citizen Leadership Training Program, 21
Clark, B., 13, 14
Codification, 43
Colin, S., 29, 57, 59, 61
Collaboration: benefits of, 20; examples of, 21–26; implications of, on leadership, 26–27; overview of, 3; in patient education programs, 80–81; and public responsibility, 19; rationale for, 20; requirements of, 20–21; strategies for, 19–21
Collaborative learning, 39
Collins, M., 9, 10, 11, 68, 78

Back Issue/Subscription Order Form

Copy or detach and send to:

Jossey-Bass, A Wiley Company, 989 Market Street, San Francisco CA 94103-1741

Call or fax toll-free: Phone 888-378-2537 6:30AM – 3PM PST; Fax 888-481-2665

Back Issues: Please send me the following issues at $29 each
(Important: please include series initials and issue number, such as ACE96.)

_____

_____

_____

$ _____ Total for single issues

$ _____ SHIPPING CHARGES: SURFACE   Domestic   Canadian

	Domestic	Canadian
First Item	$5.00	$6.00
Each Add'l Item	$3.00	$1.50

For next-day and second-day delivery rates, call the number listed above.

Subscriptions: Please __start __renew my subscription to *New Directions for Adult and Continuing Education* for the year 2____ at the following rate:

U.S.	__Individual $80	__Institutional $170
Canada	__Individual $80	__Institutional $210
All Others	__Individual $104	__Institutional $244

**For more information about online subscriptions visit
www.interscience.wiley.com**

$ _____ Total single issues and subscriptions (Add appropriate sales tax for your state for single issue orders. No sales tax for U.S. subscriptions. Canadian residents, add GST for subscriptions and single issues.)

__Payment enclosed (U.S. check or money order only)

__VISA __MC __AmEx #_____ Exp. Date _____

Signature _____ Day Phone _____

__ Bill Me (U.S. institutional orders only. Purchase order required.)

Purchase order # _____

Federal Tax ID13559302   GST 89102 8052

Name _____

Address _____

_____

Phone _____ E-mail _____

For more information about Jossey-Bass, visit our Web site at www.josseybass.com

ACE99   **Environmental Adult Education: Ecological Learning, Theory, and Practice for Socio-Environmental Change**
Darlene E. Clover, Lilian H. Hill
Situates environmental adult education within a socio-political and eco-epistemological framework, explores how new language and metaphors can counteract problematic modern worldviews, and analyzes the potential of environmental, justice-based learning to combat socio-environmental oppressions. It provides effective ways educators can connect social and ecological issues in their educational work in community, classroom, or social movements.
ISBN 0-7879-7170-7

ACE98   **New Perspectives on Designing and Implementing Professional Development of Teachers of Adults**
Kathleen P. King, Patricia A. Lawler
Explores how to make professional development more pertinent by looking at teachers of adults as adult learners themselves. It also presents an astute vision of current needs and trends, theory, and recommended practice to guide professional development in the many contexts in which teachers of adults work today—from higher education to adult literacy to corporate training.
ISBN 0-7879-6918-4

ACE97   **Accelerated Learning for Adults: The Promise and Practice of Intensive Educational Formats**
Raymond J. Wlodkowski, Carol E. Kasworm
The first major publication that addresses the current practice and research of accelerated learning formats in higher education. Contributors explore the scope of accelerated learning as it is practiced today and offer practitioner guidelines and insights for best practices in program and course design, learning strategies, and assessment approaches, as well as the integration of distance learning and service-learning into accelerated learning programs.
ISBN 0-7879-6794-7

ACE96   **Learning and Sociocultural Contexts: Implications for Adults, Community, and Workplace Education**
Mary V. Alfred
Understanding how sociocultural contexts shape the learning experience is crucial to designing, implementing, and facilitating effective learning activities with and for adults. This volume explores some of the contexts within which learning occurs and the social and cultural dynamics that influence learning and teaching. The contributors' aim is to create an awareness of the importance of context in adult learning and to encourage adult educators to be reflective of their practice, to understand how social and cultural contexts influence classroom dynamics, and to take critical action to ameliorate hegemonic practices in adult education.
ISBN 0-7879-6326-7

ACE95   **Adult Learning in Community**
Susan Imel, David Stein
Explores how adult learning occurs in naturally forming communities. As illustrated by the chapters in this volume, this learning takes a variety of forms, and in a variety of locations. It is characterized by individuals coming

together to exercise control and influence over the direction, content, and purposes of their learning and emphasizes the community or social as opposed to the individual level of learning. Although many learning communities are homogeneous in nature, several chapters reveal how power and politics play a role as well as how the presence of a facilitator can change the dynamic.
ISBN 0-7879-6323-2

ACE94   Collaborative Inquiry as a Strategy for Adult Learning
Lyle Yorks, Elizabeth Kasl
Examines the practice of collaborative inquiry (CI), a systematic process that educators can use to help adults make meaning from their experience, through richly detailed case descriptions. Highlights particular characteristics of the authors' projects so that this volume, taken as a whole, represents the diversity of issues important to adult educators. Provides guidance to adult educators while at the same time adding to the emerging discourse about this process.
ISBN 0-7879-6322-4

ACE93   Contemporary Viewpoints on Teaching Adults Effectively
Jovita Ross-Gordon
The aim of this sourcebook was to bring together several authors who have contributed through their recent publications to the recent literature on effective teaching of adults. Rather than promoting a single view of what constitutes good teaching of adults, the chapters challenge each of us to reflect on our beliefs regarding teaching and learning along with our understandings of adults learners, the teaching-learning environment, and the broader social context within which adult continuing education takes place.
ISBN 0-7879-6229-5

ACE92   Sociocultural Perspectives on Learning through Work
Tara Fenwick
Offers an introduction to current themes among academic researchers who are interested in sociocultural understandings of work-based learning and working knowledge—how people learn in and through everyday activities that they think of as work. Explores how learning is embedded in the social relationships, cultural dynamics, and politics of work, and they recommend different ways for educators to be part of the process.
ISBN 0-7879-5775-5

ACE91   Understanding and Negotiating the Political Landscape of Adult Education
Catherine A. Hansman, Peggy A. Sissel
Provides key insights into the politics and policy issues in adult education today. Offering effective strategies for reflection and action, chapters explore issues in examination and negotiation of the political aspects of higher education, adult educators in K–12-focused colleges of education, literacy education, social welfare reform, professional organizations, and identity of the field.
ISBN 0-7879-5775-5

ACE90   Promoting Journal Writing in Adult Education
Leona M. English, Marie A. Gillen
Exploring the potential for personal growth and learning through journal writing for student and mentor alike, this volume aims to establish journal writing as an integral part of the teaching and learning process. Offers

examples of how journal writing can be, and has been, integrated into educational areas as diverse as health education, higher education, education for women, and English as a Second Language.
ISBN 0-7879-5774-7

ACE89   The New Update on Adult Learning Theory
         Sharan B. Merriam
         A companion work to 1993's popular *An Update on Adult Learning Theory,*
         this issue examines the developments, research, and continuing scholarship
         in self-directed learning. Exploring context-based learning, informal and
         incidental learning, somatic learning, and narrative learning, the authors
         analyze recent additions to well-established theories and discuss the
         potential impact of today's cutting-edge approaches.
         ISBN 0-7879-5773-9

ACE88   Strategic Use of Learning Technologies
         Elizabeth J. Burge
         The contributors draw on case examples to explore the advantages and
         disadvantages of three existing learning technologies—print, radio, and the
         Internet—and examine how a large urban university has carefully combined
         old and new technologies to provide a range of learner services tailored to its
         enormous and varied student body.
         ISBN 0-7879-5426-8

ACE87   Team Teaching and Learning in Adult Education
         Mary-Jane Eisen, Elizabeth J. Tisdell
         The contributors show how team teaching can increase both organizational
         and individual learning in settings outside of a traditional classroom, for
         example, a recently deregulated public utility, a national literacy
         organization, and community-based settings such as Chicago's south side.
         They discuss how team teaching can be used in colleges and universities,
         describing strategies for administrators and teachers who want to integrate it
         into their curricula and classrooms.
         ISBN 0-7879-5425-X

ACE86   Charting a Course for Continuing Professional Education: Reframing
         Professional Practice
         Vivian W. Mott, Barbara J. Daley
         This volume offers a resource to help practitioners examine and improve
         professional practice, and set new directions for the field of CPE across
         multiple professions. The contributors provide a brief review of the
         development of the field of CPE, analyze significant issues and trends that are
         shaping and changing the field, and propose a vision of the future of CPE.
         ISBN 0-7879-5424-1

ACE85   Addressing the Spiritual Dimensions of Adult Learning: What Educators
         Can Do
         Leona M. English, Marie A. Gillen
         The contributors discuss how mentoring, self-directed learning, and
         dialogue can be used to promote spiritual development, and advocate the
         learning covenant as a way of formalizing the sanctity of the bond between
         learners and educators. Drawing on examples from continuing professional
         education, community development, and health education, they show how a
         spiritual dimension has been integrated into adult education programs.
         ISBN 0-7879-5364-4

ACE84 An Update on Adult Development Theory: New Ways of Thinking About
the Life Course
M. Carolyn Clark, Rosemary J. Caffarella
This volume presents discussions of well-established theories and new
perspectives on learning in adulthood. Knowles' andragogy, self-directed
learning, Mezirow's perspective transformation, and several other models are
assessed for their contribution to our understanding of adult learning. In
addition, recent theoretical orientations, including consciousness and
learning, situated cognition, critical theory, and feminist pedagogy, are
discussed in terms of how each expands the knowledge base of adult
learning.
ISBN 0-7879-1171-2

ACE83 The Welfare-to-Work Challenge for Adult Literacy Educators
Larry G. Martin, James C. Fisher
Welfare reform and workforce development legislation has had a dramatic
impact on the funding, implementation, and evaluation of adult basic
education and literacy programs. This issue provides a framework for
literacy practitioners to better align their field with the demands of the Work
First environment and to meet the pragmatic expectations of an extended
list of stakeholders.
ISBN 0-7879-1170-4

ACE82 Providing Culturally Relevant Adult Education: A Challenge for the
Twenty-First Century
Talmadge C. Guy
This issue offers more inclusive theories that focus on how learners
construct meaning in a social and cultural context. Chapters identify ways
that adult educators can work more effectively with racially, ethnically, and
linguistically marginalized learners, and explore how adult education can be
an effective tool for empowering learners to take control of their
circumstances.
ISBN 0-7879-1167-4

ACE79 The Power and Potential of Collaborative Learning Partnerships
Iris M. Saltiel, Angela Sgroi, Ralph G. Brockett
This volume draws on examples of collaborative partnerships to explore the
many ways collaboration can generate learning and knowledge. The
contributors identify the factors that make for strong collaborative
relationships, and they reveal how these partnerships actually help learners
generate knowledge and insights well beyond what each brings to the
learning situation.
ISBN 0-7879-9815-X

ACE77 Using Learning to Meet the Challenges of Older Adulthood
James C. Fisher, Mary Alice Wolf
Combining theory and research in educational gerontology with the practice
of older adult learning and education, this volume explores issues related to
older adult education in academic and community settings. It is designed for
educators and others concerned with the phenomenon of aging in America
and with the continuing development of the field of educational
gerontology.
ISBN 0-7879-1164-X

ACE75 Assessing Adult Learning in Diverse Settings: Current Issues and Approaches
Amy D. Rose, Meredyth A. Leahy
Examines assessment approaches analytically from different programmatic levels and looks at the implications of these differing approaches. Chapters discuss the implications of cultural differences as well as ideas about knowledge and knowing and the implications these ideas can have for both the participant and the program.
ISBN 0-7879-9840-0

ACE70 A Community-Based Approach to Literacy Programs: Taking Learners' Lives into Account
Peggy A. Sissel
Encouraging a community-based approach that takes account of the reality of learner's lives, this volume offers suggestions for incorporating knowledge about a learner's particular context, culture, and community into adult literacy programming.
ISBN 0-7879-9867-2

ACE69 What Really Matters in Adult Education Program Planning: Lessons in Negotiating Power and Interests
Ronald M. Cervero, Arthur L. Wilson
Identifies issues faced by program planners in practice settings and the actual negotiation strategies they use. Argues that planning is generally conducted within a set of personal, organizational, and social relationships among people who may have similar, different, or conflicting interests and the program planner's responsibility centers on how to negotiate these interests to construct an effective program.
ISBN 0-7879-9866-4

ACE66 Mentoring: New Strategies and Challenges
Michael W. Galbraith, Norman H. Cohen
Assists educators in clarifying and describing various elements of the mentoring process. Also intended to enhance the reader's understanding of the utility, practice application, and research potential of mentoring in adult and continuing education.
ISBN 0-7879-9912-1

ACE59 Applying Cognitive Learning Theory to Adult Learning
Daniele D. Flannery
While much is written about adult learning, basic tenets of cognitive theory are often taken for granted. This volume presents an understanding of basic cognitive theory and applies it to the teaching-learning exchange.
ISBN 1-55542-716-2

ACE57 An Update on Adult Learning Theory
Sharan B. Merriam
This volume presents discussions of well-established theories and new perspectives on learning in adulthood. Knowles' andragogy, self-directed learning, Mezirow's perspective transformation, and several other models are assessed for their contribution to our understanding of adult learning.
ISBN 1-55542-684-0

NEW DIRECTIONS FOR
ADULT AND CONTINUING EDUCATION
IS NOW AVAILABLE ONLINE AT WILEY INTERSCIENCE

What is Wiley InterScience?

Wiley InterScience is the dynamic online content service from John Wiley & Sons delivering the full text of over 300 leading scientific, technical, medical, and professional journals, plus major reference works, the acclaimed *Current Protocols* laboratory manuals, and even the full text of select Wiley print books online.

What are some special features of Wiley InterScience?

Wiley InterScience Alerts is a service that delivers table of contents via e-mail for any journal available on Wiley InterScience as soon as a new issue is published online.

Early View is Wiley's exclusive service presenting individual articles online as soon as they are ready, even before the release of the compiled print issue. These articles are complete, peer-reviewed, and citable.

CrossRef is the innovative multi-publisher reference linking system enabling readers to move seamlessly from a reference in a journal article to the cited publication, typically located on a different server and published by a different publisher.

How can I access Wiley InterScience?

Visit http://www.interscience.wiley.com

Guest Users can browse Wiley InterScience for unrestricted access to journal Tables of Contents and Article Abstracts, or use the powerful search engine. *Registered Users* are provided with a *Personal Home Page* to store and manage customized alerts, searches, and links to favorite journals and articles. Additionally, Registered Users can view free Online Sample Issues and preview selected material from major reference works. *Licensed Customers* are entitled to access full-text journal articles in PDF, with select journals also offering full-text HTML.

How do I become an Authorized User?

Authorized Users are individuals authorized by a paying Customer to have access to the journals in Wiley InterScience. For example, a university that subscribes to Wiley journals is considered to be the Customer. Faculty, staff and students authorized by the university to have access to those journals in Wiley InterScience are Authorized Users. Users should contact their Library for information on which Wiley journals they have access to in Wiley InterScience.

ASK YOUR INSTITUTION ABOUT WILEY INTERSCIENCE TODAY!

Statement of Ownership, Management, and Circulation

1. Publication Title	2. Publication Number								3. Filing Date
New Directions For Adult & Continuing Education	1	0	5	2	_	2	8	9	1	10/1/04

4. Issue Frequency	5. Number of Issues Published Annually	6. Annual Subscription Price
Quarterly	4	$170.00

7. Complete Mailing Address of Known Office of Publication (Not printer) (Street, city, county, state, and ZIP+4)	Contact Person
Wiley Subscription Services, Inc. at Jossey-Bass, 989 Market Street, San Francisco, CA 94103	Joe Schuman
	Telephone (415) 782-3232

8. Complete Mailing Address of Headquarters or General Business Office of Publisher (Not printer)

Wiley Subscription Services, Inc. 111 River Street, Hoboken, NJ 07030

9. Full Names and Complete Mailing Addresses of Publisher, Editor, and Managing Editor (Do not leave blank)

Publisher (Name and complete mailing address)

Wiley, San Francisco, 989 Market Street, San Francisco, CA 94103-1741

Editor (Name and complete mailing address)

Susan Imel, Ohio State University/Eric-Acve, 1900 Kenny Road, Columbus, OH 43210-1090

Managing Editor (Name and complete mailing address)

None

10. Owner (Do not leave blank. If the publication is owned by a corporation, give the name and address of the corporation immediately followed by the names and addresses of all stockholders owning or holding 1 percent or more of the total amount of stock. If not owned by a corporation, give the names and addresses of the individual owners. If owned by a partnership or other unincorporated firm, give its name and address as well as those of each individual owner. If the publication is published by a nonprofit organization, give its name and address.)

Full Name	Complete Mailing Address
Wiley Subscription Services, Inc.	111 River Street, Hoboken, NJ 07030
(see attached list)	

11. Known Bondholders, Mortgagees, and Other Security Holders Owning or Holding 1 Percent or More of Total Amount of Bonds, Mortgages, or Other Securities. If none, check box ➤ ☑ None

Full Name	Complete Mailing Address
None	None

12. Tax Status (For completion by nonprofit organizations authorized to mail at nonprofit rates) (Check one)
The purpose, function, and nonprofit status of this organization and the exempt status for federal income tax purposes:
☐ Has Not Changed During Preceding 12 Months
☐ Has Changed During Preceding 12 Months (Publisher must submit explanation of change with this statement)

PS Form **3526**, October 1999   (See Instructions on Reverse)

13. Publication Title New Directions For Adult & Continuing Education	14. Issue Date for Circulation Data Below Summer 2004

15. Extent and Nature of Circulation		Average No. Copies Each Issue During Preceding 12 Months	No. Copies of Single Issue Published Nearest to Filing Date
a. Total Number of Copies (Net press run)		1539	1629
b. Paid and/or Requested Circulation	(1) Paid/Requested Outside-County Mail Subscriptions Stated on Form 3541. (Include advertiser's proof and exchange copies)	572	551
	(2) Paid In-County Subscriptions Stated on Form 3541 (Include advertiser's proof and exchange copies)	0	0
	(3) Sales Through Dealers and Carriers, Street Vendors, Counter Sales, and Other Non-USPS Paid Distribution	0	0
	(4) Other Classes Mailed Through the USPS	0	0
c. Total Paid and/or Requested Circulation [Sum of 15b. (1), (2),(3),and (4)] ➤		572	551
d. Free Distribution by Mail (Samples, complimentary, and other free)	(1) Outside-County as Stated on Form 3541	59	48
	(2) In-County as Stated on Form 3541	0	0
	(3) Other Classes Mailed Through the USPS	0	0
e. Free Distribution Outside the Mail (Carriers or other means)		0	0
f. Total Free Distribution (Sum of 15d. and 15e.) ➤		59	48
g. Total Distribution (Sum of 15c. and 15f) ➤		631	599
h. Copies not Distributed		908	1030
i. Total (Sum of 15g. and h.) ➤		1539	1629
j. Percent Paid and/or Requested Circulation (15c. divided by 15g. times 100)		91%	91%

16. Publication of Statement of Ownership
☑ Publication required. Will be printed in the **Winter 2004** issue of this publication. ☐ Publication not required.

17. Signature and Title of Editor, Publisher, Business Manager, or Owner | Date

Susan E. Lewis, VP & Publisher - Periodicals   *Susan E. Lewis*   10/01/04

I certify that all information furnished on this form is true and complete. I understand that anyone who furnishes false or misleading information on this form or who omits material or information requested on the form may be subject to criminal sanctions (including fines and imprisonment) and/or civil sanctions (including civil penalties).